Oh! My Grammar 2

CEDUBOOK

Unit Components

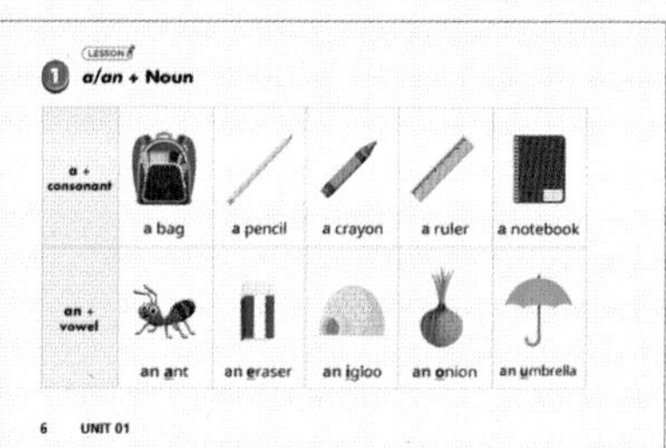

- **LISTEN & CIRCLE**
  LISTEN & SAY

Fun and authentic context helps students to easily understand how to use the grammar in real life.

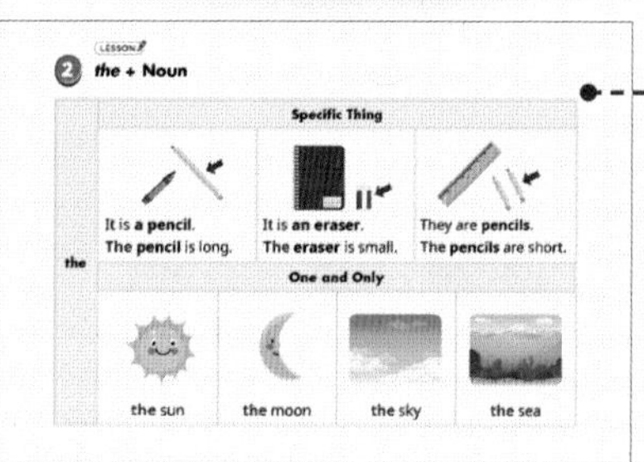

- **GRAMMAR POINT**

Students can learn the target grammar through easy-to-read tables and colorful illustrations with clear examples.

- **LET'S PRACTICE**

Various kinds of exercises and drills are designed to develop students' understanding of the grammar they learned. These will also gradually encourage students to apply the forms accurately.

- **LET'S WRITE**

The extended writing activity encourages students to use the language more productively in a variety of contexts.

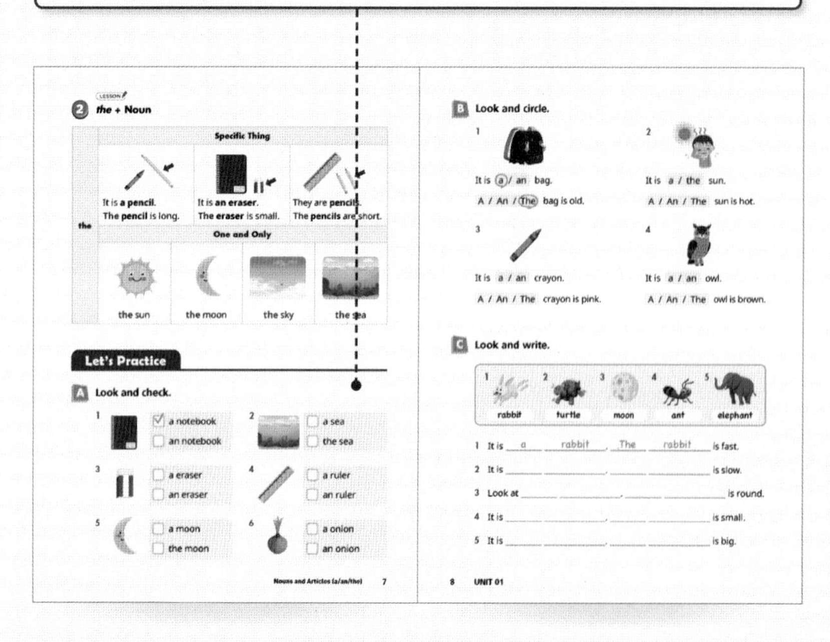

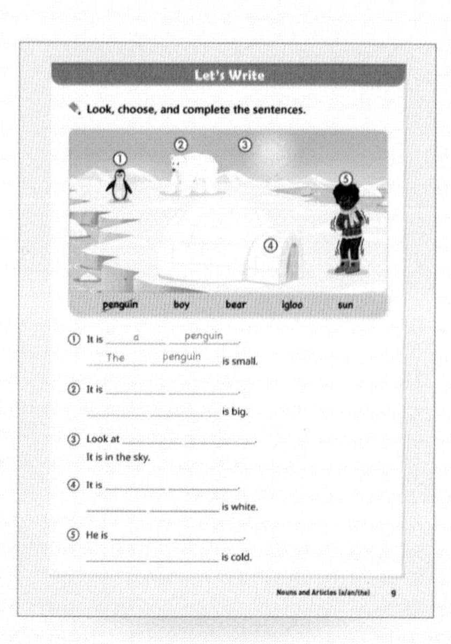

• REVIEW

The review sections help students to recall the language they learned in the previous three to four units. They also allow students to evaluate their understanding of the grammar.

• MINI TEST

The mini test is a cumulative review incorporating the previous seven to eight units. Students will be able to differentiate the grammar points they learned and use them appropriately.

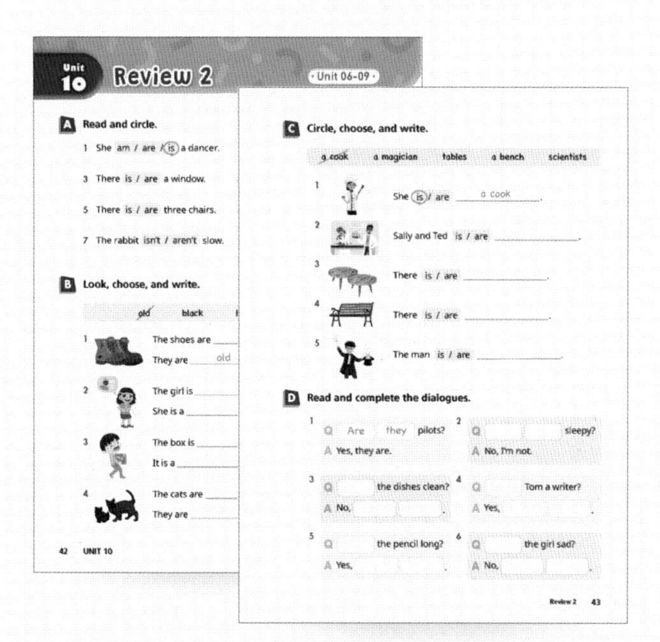

Unit 10 Review 2 · Unit 06-09 ·

A Read and circle.

1 She am / are / is a dancer.

3 There is / are a window.

5 There is / are three chairs.

7 The rabbit isn't / aren't slow.

B Look, choose, and write.

old black

1 The shoes are ___ They are old

2 The girl is ___ She is a ___

3 The box is ___ It is a ___

4 The cats are ___ They are ___

42 UNIT 10

C Circle, choose, and write.

a cook a magician tables a bench scientists

1 She is / are a cook.

2 Sally and Ted is / are ___

3 There is / are ___

4 There is / are ___

5 The man is / are ___

D Read and complete the dialogues.

1 Q Are they pilots? A Yes, they are.

2 Q ___ sleepy? A No, I'm not.

3 Q ___ the dishes clean? A No, ___

4 Q ___ Tom a writer? A Yes, ___

5 Q ___ the pencil long? A Yes, ___

6 Q ___ the girl sad? A No, ___

Review 2 43

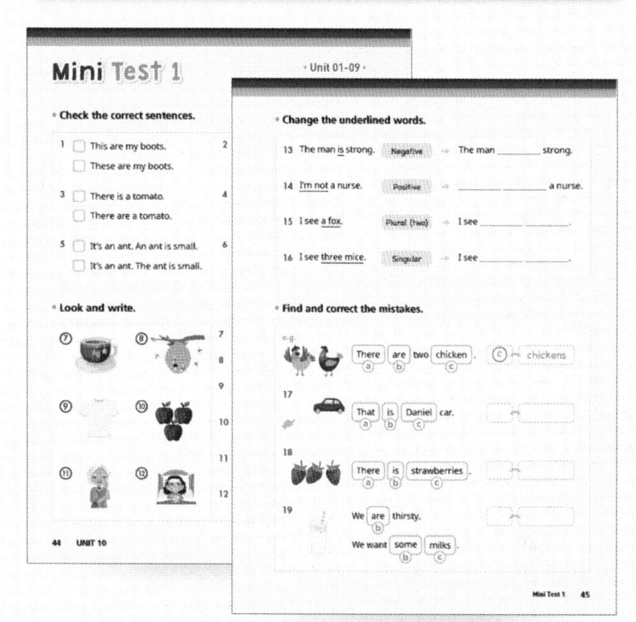

Mini Test 1 · Unit 01-09 ·

• Check the correct sentences.

1 This are my boots. / These are my boots.

3 There is a tomato. / There are a tomato.

5 It's an ant. An ant is small. / It's an ant. The ant is small.

• Look and write.

44 UNIT 10

• Change the underlined words.

13 The man is strong. Negative → The man ___ strong.

14 I'm not a nurse. Positive → ___ a nurse.

15 I see a fox. Plural (two) → I see ___.

16 I see three mice. Singular → I see ___.

• Find and correct the mistakes.

e.g. There are two chicken. ⓒ → chickens

17 That is Daniel car.

18 There is strawberries.

19 We are thirsty. We want some milks.

Mini Test 1 45

FREE GRAMMAR LESSON

Friendly and detailed grammar audio lessons in Korean are provided to help students comprehend the grammar points more easily.

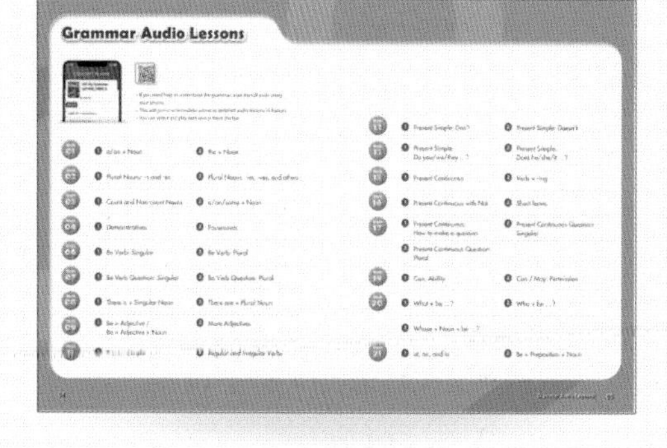

Grammar Audio Lessons

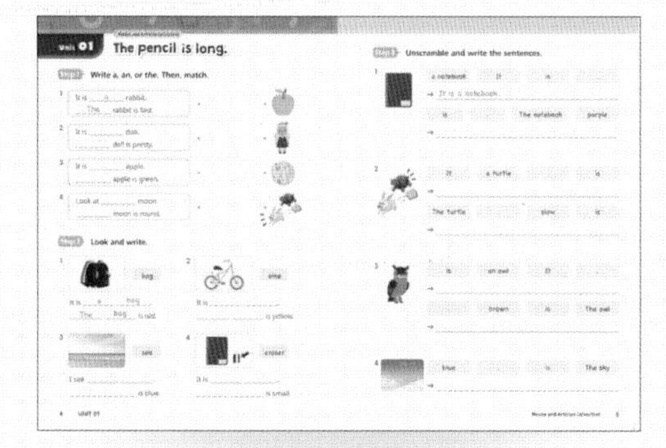

Unit 01 The pencil is long.

WORKBOOK

Each unit consists of three steps of writing exercises.
These are designed to develop students' sentence building skills.
They can reinforce their writing skills and gain confidence by completing the exercises.

Contents

Nouns & Others

Be Verbs & More

Present Simple

Present Continuous

Modal Verbs & Others

Nouns and Articles (a/an/the)

Unit 01 The pencil is long.

✦ Listen and circle.

LESSON

1 a/an + Noun

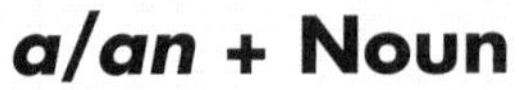

a + consonant	**a** bag	**a** pencil	**a** crayon	**a** ruler	**a** notebook
an + vowel	**an** ant	**an** eraser	**an** igloo	**an** onion	**an** umbrella

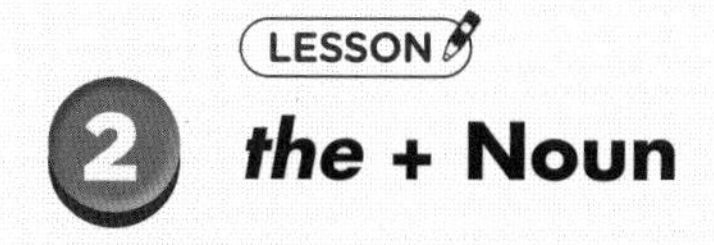

LESSON 2 *the* + Noun

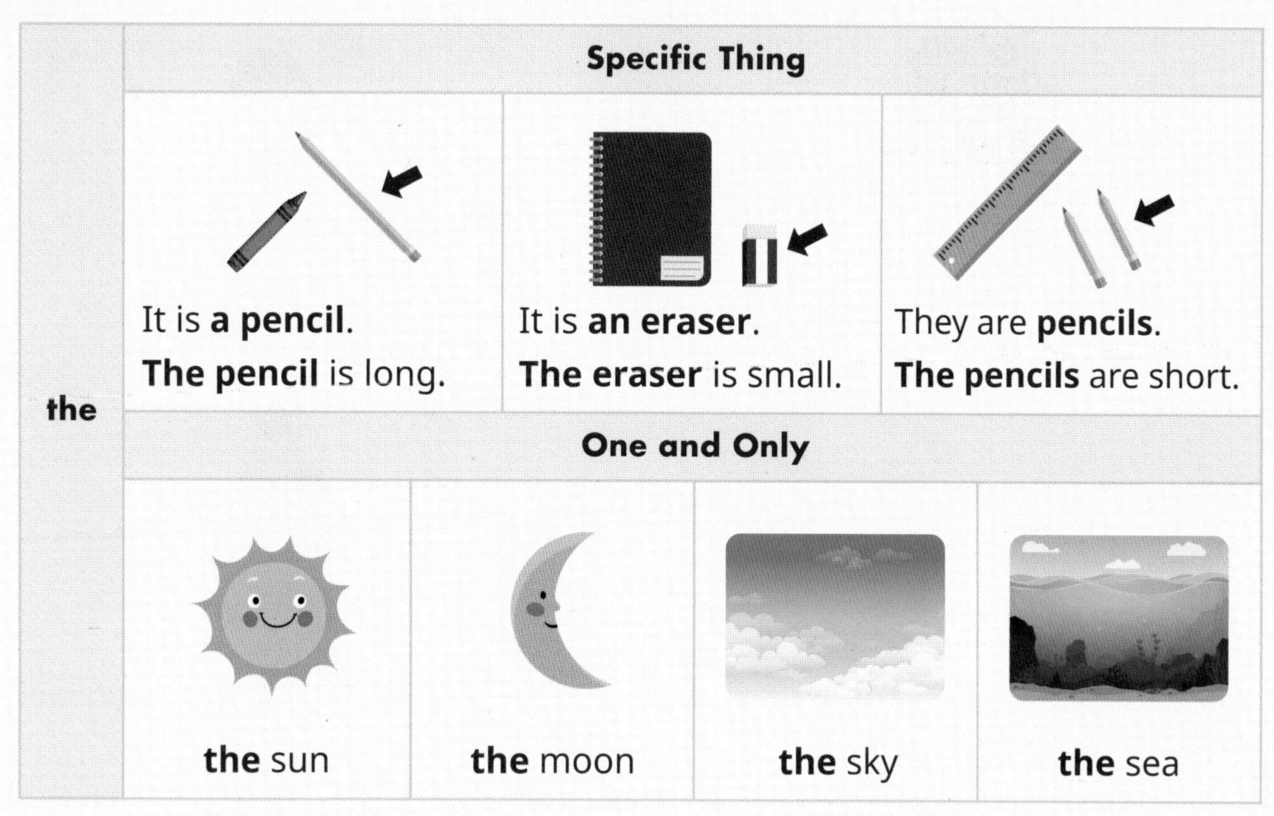

	Specific Thing			
the	It is **a pencil**. **The pencil** is long.	It is **an eraser**. **The eraser** is small.	They are **pencils**. **The pencils** are short.	
	One and Only			
	the sun	**the** moon	**the** sky	**the** sea

Let's Practice

A Look and check.

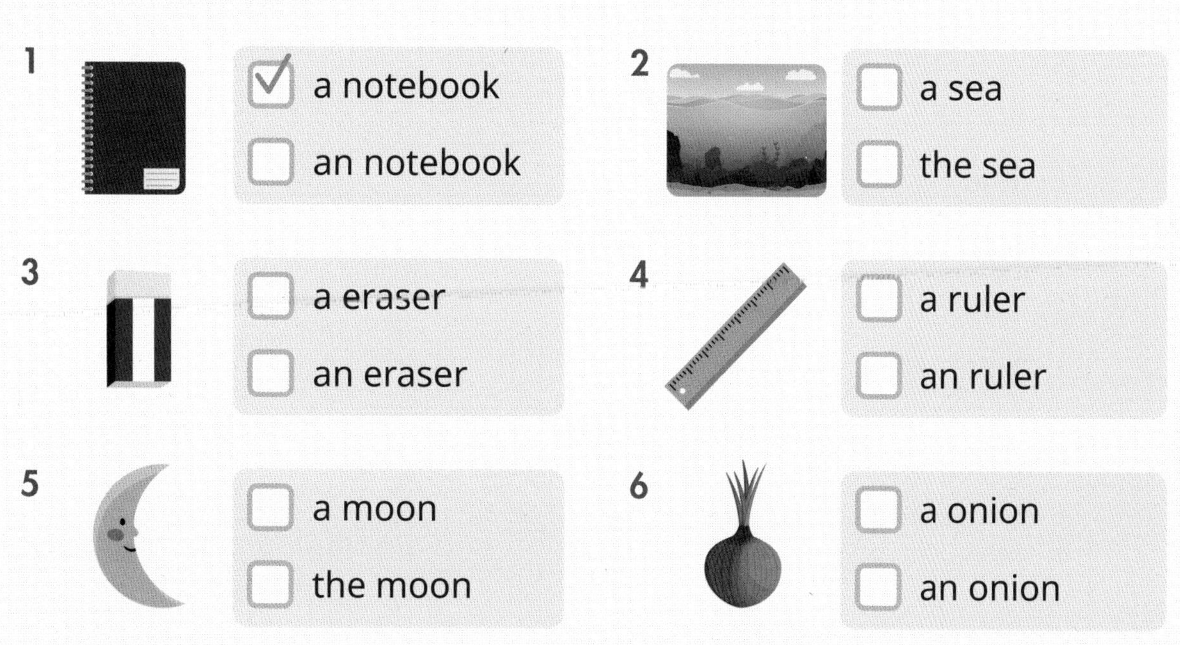

1. ☑ a notebook ☐ an notebook
2. ☐ a sea ☐ the sea
3. ☐ a eraser ☐ an eraser
4. ☐ a ruler ☐ an ruler
5. ☐ a moon ☐ the moon
6. ☐ a onion ☐ an onion

B Look and circle.

1

It is a / an bag.

A / An / The bag is old.

2

It is a / the sun.

A / An / The sun is hot.

3

It is a / an crayon.

A / An / The crayon is pink.

4

It is a / an owl.

A / An / The owl is brown.

C Look and write.

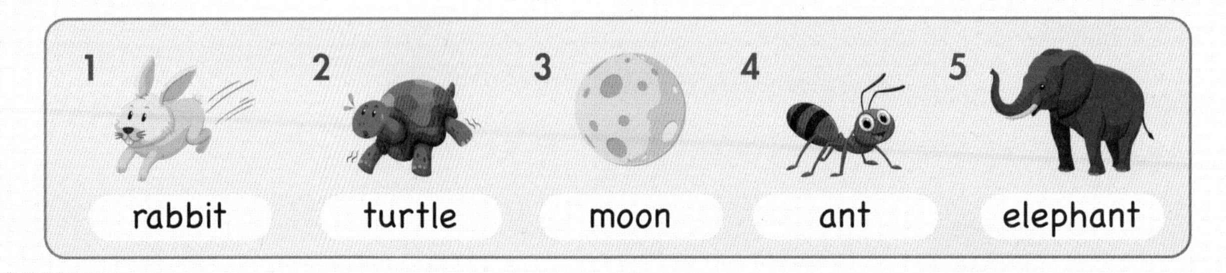

1 It is ___a___ ___rabbit___. ___The___ ___rabbit___ is fast.

2 It is ______ ______. ______ ______ is slow.

3 Look at ______ ______. ______ ______ is round.

4 It is ______ ______. ______ ______ is small.

5 It is ______ ______. ______ ______ is big.

Let's Write

Look, choose, and complete the sentences.

① It is ___a___ ___penguin___.

___The___ ___penguin___ is small.

② It is ______ ______.

______ ______ is big.

③ Look at ______ ______.

It is in the sky.

④ It is ______ ______.

______ ______ is white.

⑤ He is ______ ______.

______ ______ is cold.

Plural Nouns

Unit 02 They are puppies.

✦ Listen and circle.

1 Plural Nouns: *-s* and *-es*

-s	a chicken	chicken**s**	a tree	tree**s**
-es	a pea<u>**ch**</u>	peach**es**	a bru<u>**sh**</u>	brush**es**
	a glas<u>s</u>	glass**es**	a bo<u>**x**</u>	box**es**

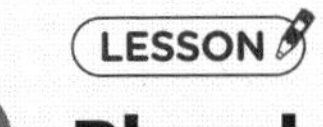

2 Plural Nouns: *-ies*, *-ves*, and *others*

-ies	a bab**y**	bab**ies**	a pupp**y**	pupp**ies**
-ves	a wol**f**	wol**ves**	a kni**fe**	kni**ves**
others	a foot	f**ee**t	a man	m**e**n
	a child	child**ren**	a mouse	m**ice**

A Look and circle.

1 horses / horsees

2 boxs / boxes

3 mice / mouses

4 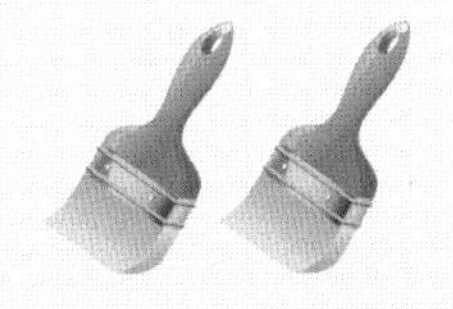

brushs / brushes

5 knifes / knives

6 puppys / puppies

B Choose and write the plural nouns.

~~bag~~ man tree glass leaf bench puppy

-s	-es	-ies	-ves	others
bags	________	________	________	________
________	________			

C Look, choose, and write.

~~chicken~~ child baby foot dress scarf

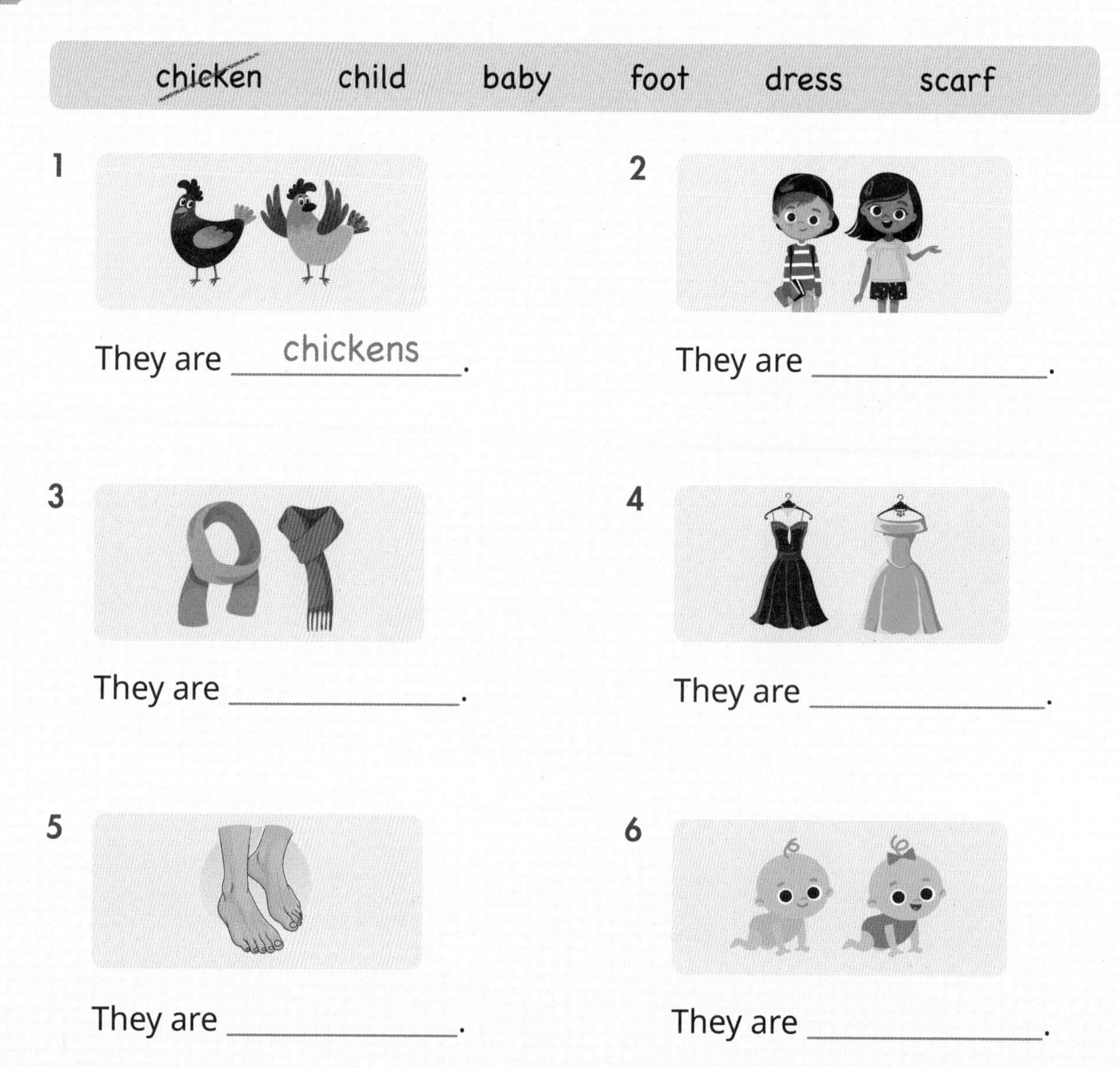

1 They are chickens.

2 They are __________.

3 They are __________.

4 They are __________.

5 They are __________.

6 They are __________.

Let's Write

Look, choose, and complete the sentences.

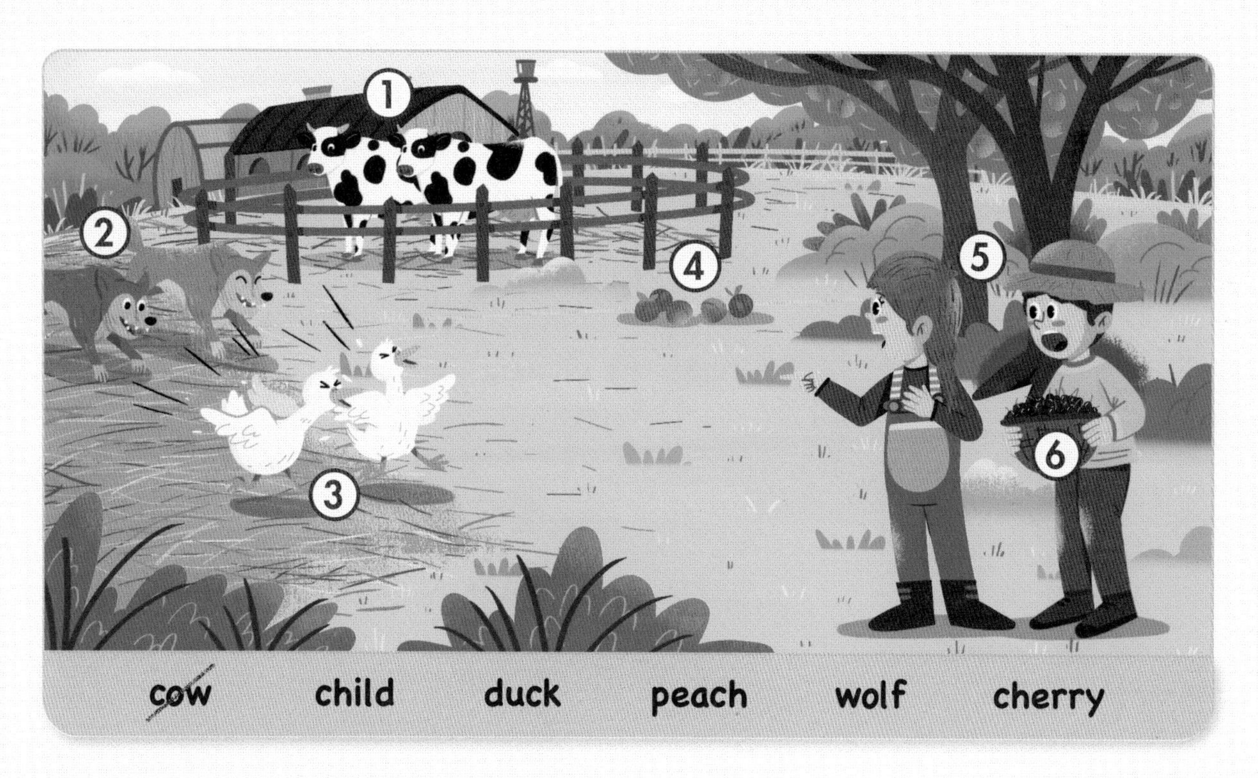

① They are cows.

② They are ____________.

③ They are ____________.

④ They are ____________.

⑤ They are ____________.

⑥ They are ____________.

Count and Non-count Nouns

Unit 03 I want bread.

✦ Listen and say.

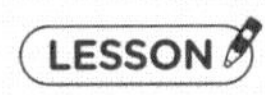

1 Count and Non-count Nouns

Count Nouns		Non-count Nouns	
a cookie	two cookie**s**	bread	cheese
an orange	three orange**s**	juice	water

2 *a/an/some* + Noun

Count Nouns			Non-count Nouns	
Singular	Plural			
a/an	-	some	-	some
a peach	two peach**es**	**some** peach**es**	bread	**some** bread
an egg	six egg**s**	**some** egg**s**	cheese	**some** cheese

Let's Practice

A Can you count it? Write Yes(*Y*) or No(*N*).

1	strawberry	Y	2	water	
3	tea		4	egg	
5	cheese		6	cup	
7	cookie		8	salt	

B Look and circle.

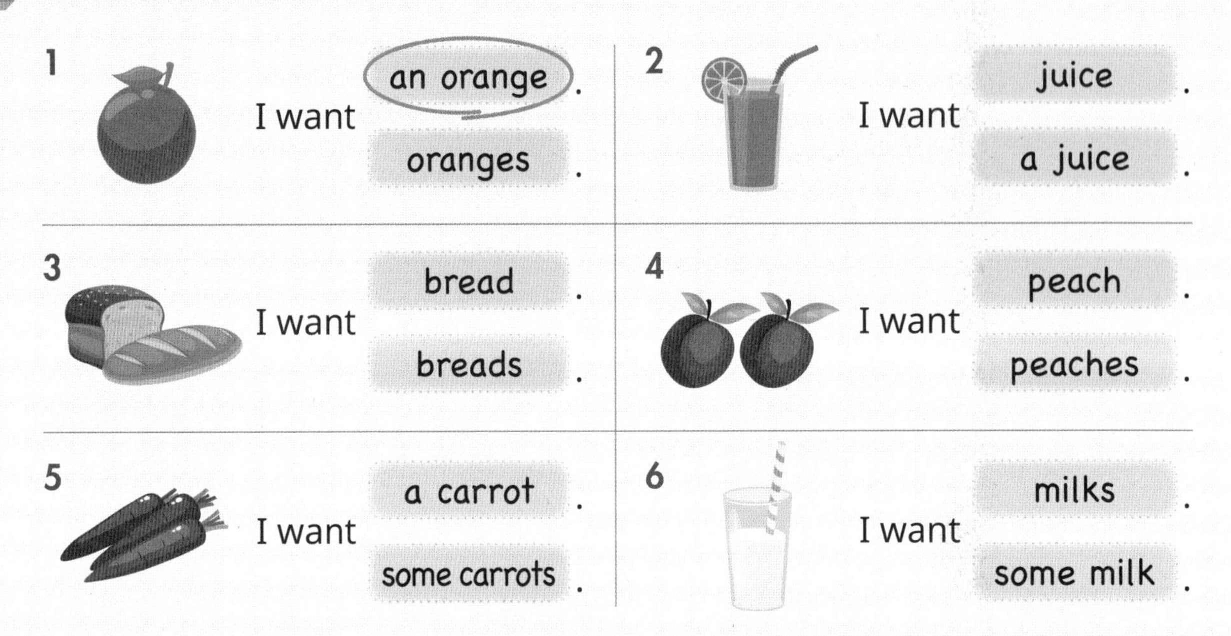

C Look and write *a*, *an*, or *some*.

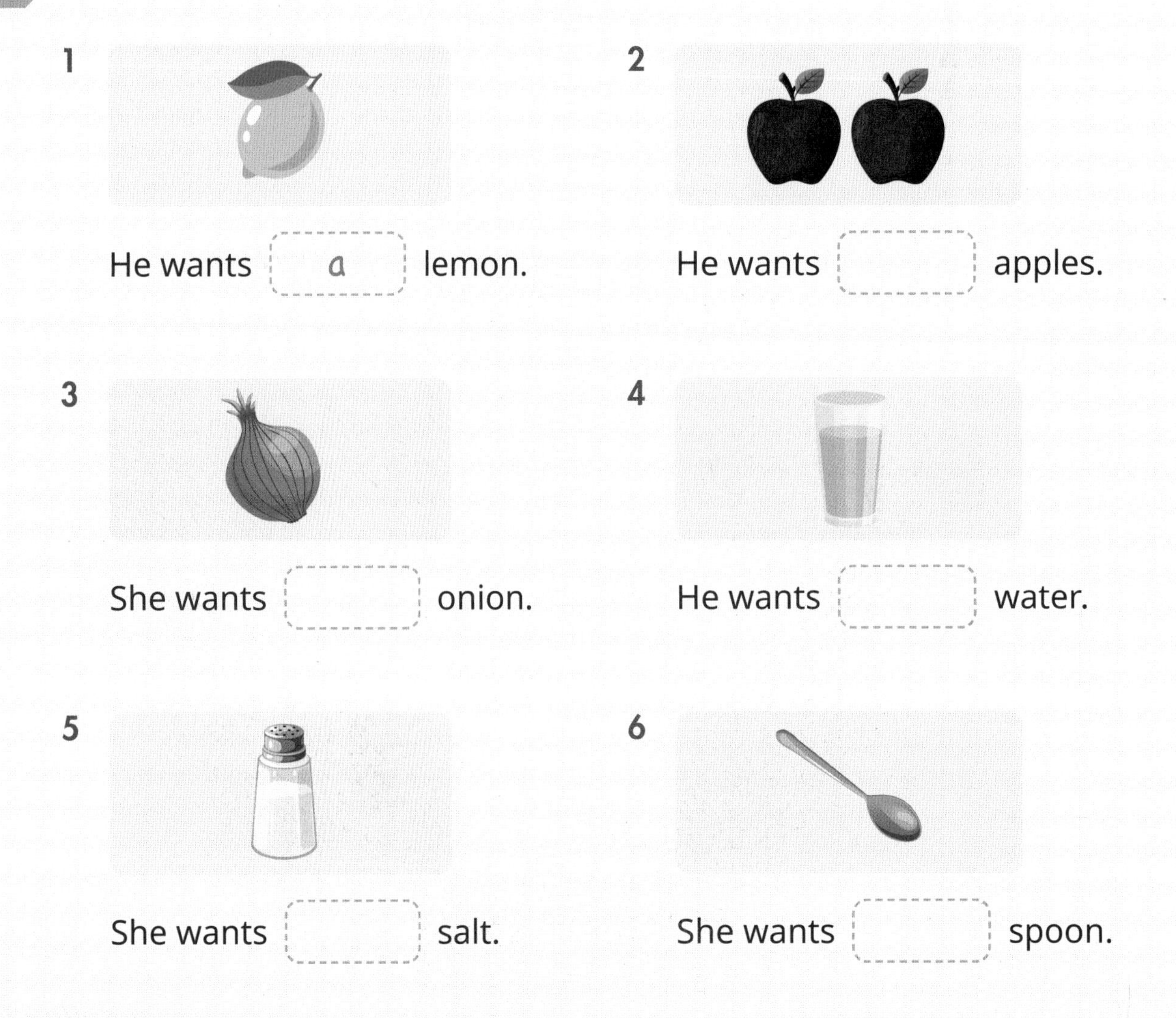

Let's Write

Look and write with *a*, *an*, or *some*.

Cindy

① Cindy wants some eggs.

② Cindy wants ______ ______.

③ Cindy wants ______ ______.

Eric

④ Eric wants ______ ______.

⑤ Eric wants ______ ______.

⑥ Eric wants ______ ______.

⑦ Eric wants ______ ______.

Demonstratives and Possessives

Unit 04 This is my watch.

Listen and circle.

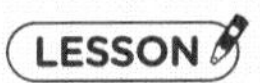

1 Demonstratives: *This, That / These, Those*

LESSON

2 Possessives

Pronoun	Possessive
I	**my**
you	**your**
he	**his**
she	**her**
it	**its**
we	**our**
they	**their**

Noun	Possessive
Anna	**Anna's**
dog	**dog's**
Alex and Ken	**Alex and Ken's**

I have a watch.
This is **my** watch.

He has gloves.
These are **his** gloves.

We have a pet.
That is **our** pet.

They have cars.
Those are **their** cars.

Sue has a scarf.
That is **Sue's** scarf.

The cat has a fish.
This is **the cat's** fish.

Let's Practice

A Look and circle.

1 This / That is my desk.

2 This / That is my bed.

3 These / Those are my pets.

B Look and write.

1 **He** has shoes.
These are [his] shoes.

2 **We** have a house.
This is [ ] house.

3 **They** have bikes.
Those are [ ] bikes.

4 **She** has a car.
That is [ ] car.

C Look and write.

1

That is Luna's scarf.
[Luna]

2

__________ is __________ book.
[you]

3

__________ are __________ gifts.
[she]

4

__________ is __________ cat.
[Tom]

5

__________ are __________ gloves.
[I]

6

__________ is __________ school.
[we]

Let's Write

They go outside in the winter. Look, choose, and write.

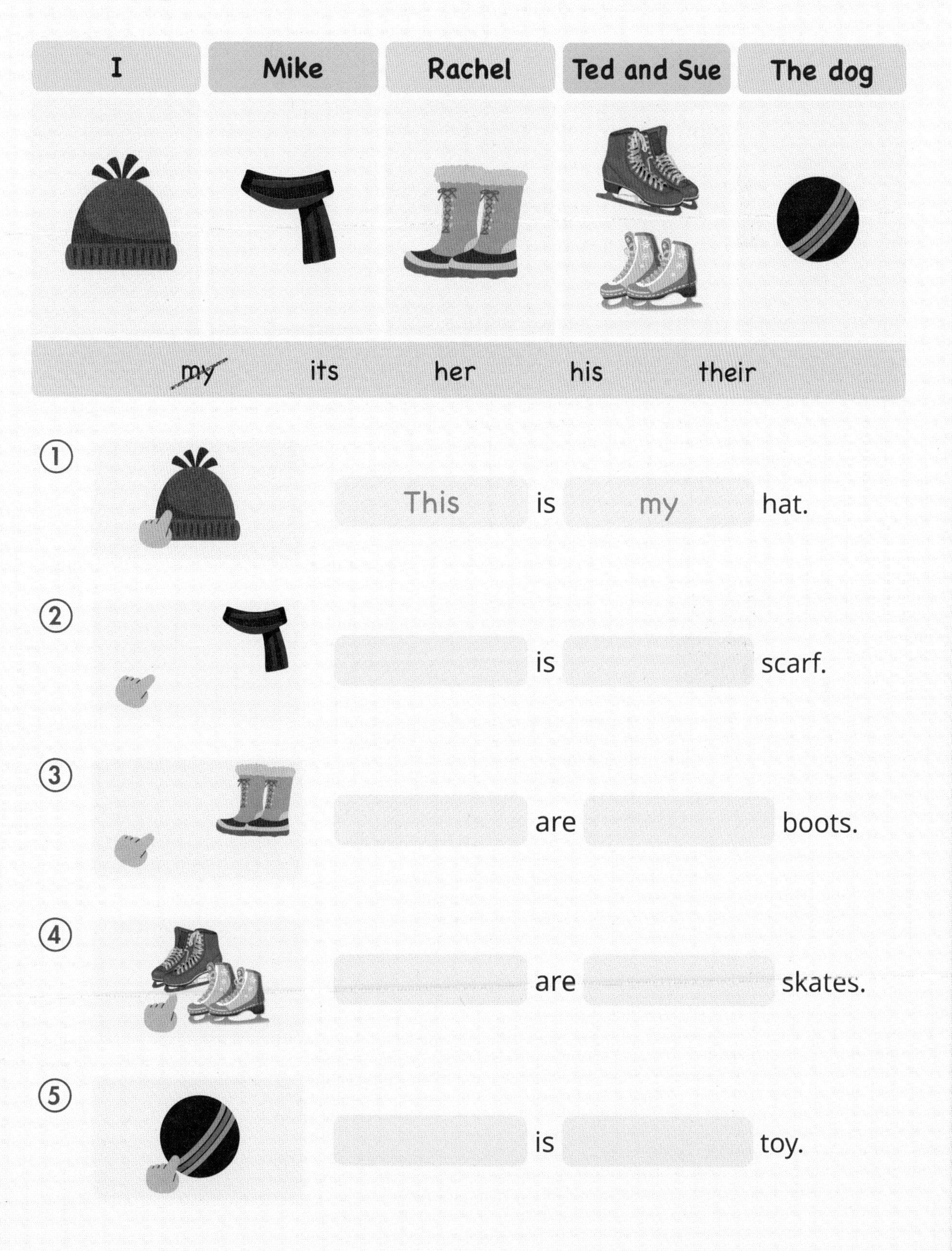

Review 1

A Look and check.

1

- [ ] It is a owl.
- [x] It is an owl.

2

- [ ] He wants milk.
- [ ] He wants a milk.

3

- [ ] Look at the puppys.
- [ ] Look at the puppies.

4

- [ ] It is a bag. A bag is old.
- [ ] It is a bag. The bag is old.

B Read and circle.

1 They are peachs / (peaches).

2 A / The sky is gray.

3 This is Amy / Amy's scarf.

4 Mike wants a / some juice.

5 Those are I / my boots.

6 I have two feet / foots.

7 It is an onion / carrot.

8 He has cheese / a cheese.

C Look, choose, and write.

~~a~~	an	the	some	her	his

1 It is ___a___ turtle. The turtle is slow.

2 He wants ______ bread.

3 Amy has a bike. It is ______ bike.

4 Look at ______ moon.

5 It is ______ egg. The egg is small.

6 Tom has shoes. They are ______ shoes.

D Write the plural nouns.

1 horse ······ They are ___horses___.

2 wolf ······ They are ______.

3 child ······ I see some ______.

4 cherry ······ She wants some ______.

5 glass ······ They have three ______.

E Look and write.

1

They are boxes.

2

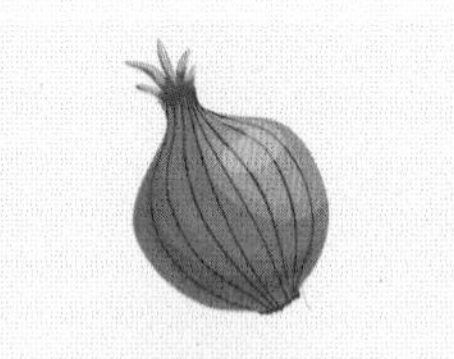

It is __________ onion.

3

__________ are your gifts.

4

He wants __________ water.

5

I see two __________.

6

They are __________.

7

__________ is our house.

8

__________ are their bikes.

9

It is an elephant.

__________ elephant is big.

10

I have a peach.

I have __________ apples.

Correct the mistakes.

1 They are brushs. → brushes

2 This is Andy cat. → 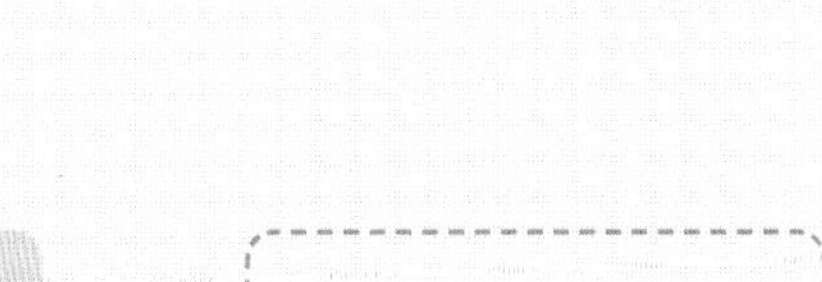

3 He has an watch. → 

4 She wants a juice. → 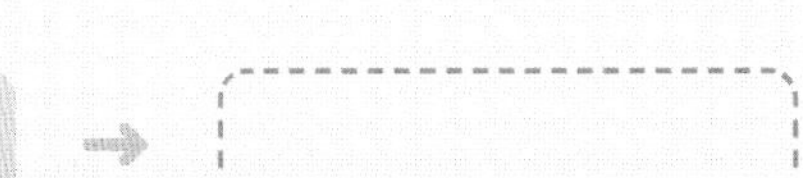

5  I see two mans. → 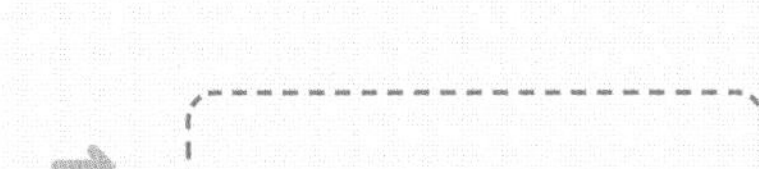 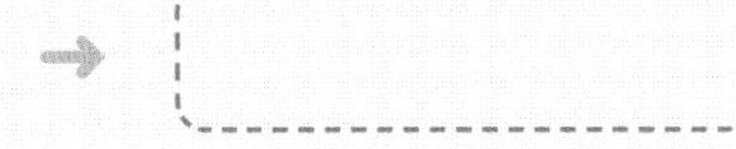

6  These are you gloves. → 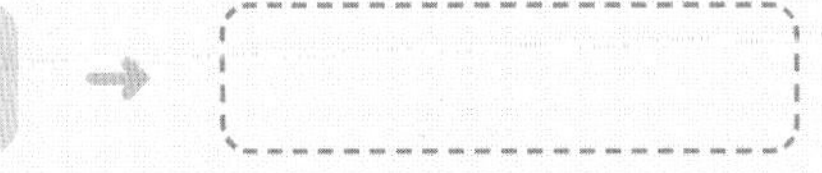

7  I want some cookie. → 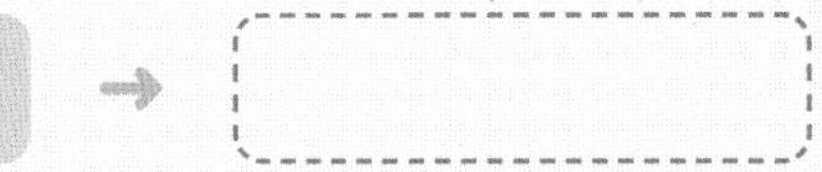

Be Verb: Positives and Negatives

She is a singer.

✦ Listen and circle.

LESSON

1 Be Verb: Singular

Positive		Negative	
I **am**	I**'m**	I **am not**	I**'m not**
You **are**	You**'re**	You **are not**	You **aren't**
He / She / It **is**	He**'s** / She**'s** / It**'s**	He / She / It **is not**	He / She / It **isn't**

I **am** a painter.
I**'m not** a writer.

You **are** a singer.
You **aren't** a pianist.

He **is** a magician.
He **isn't** an actor.

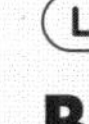

LESSON

2 Be Verb: Plural

Positive		Negative	
We **are**	We**'re**	We **are not**	We **aren't**
You **are**	You**'re**	You **are not**	You **aren't**
They **are**	They**'re**	They **are not**	They **aren't**

We **are** painters.
We **aren't** writers.

You **are** singers.
You **aren't** pianists.

They **are** magicians.
They **aren't** actors.

Let's Practice

A Look and circle.

① 

②

③ 

④

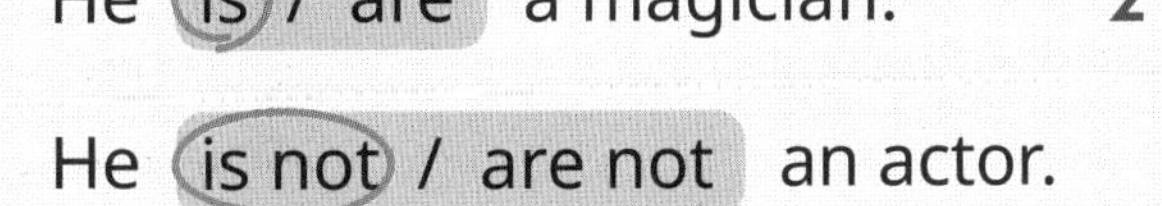

1 He is / are a magician.
He is not / are not an actor.

2 I are / am a cook.
I are not / am not a doctor.

3 Chris is / are a bus driver.
He is not / are not a pilot.

4 They is / are singers.
They is not / are not painters.

B Write the short forms.

1 They are wolves. → They're wolves.

2 She is a magician. → ______ a magician.

3 I am a writer. → ______ a writer.

4 He is not an actor. → ______ ______ an actor.

5 We are not painters. → ______ ______ painters.

C Look, choose, and write.

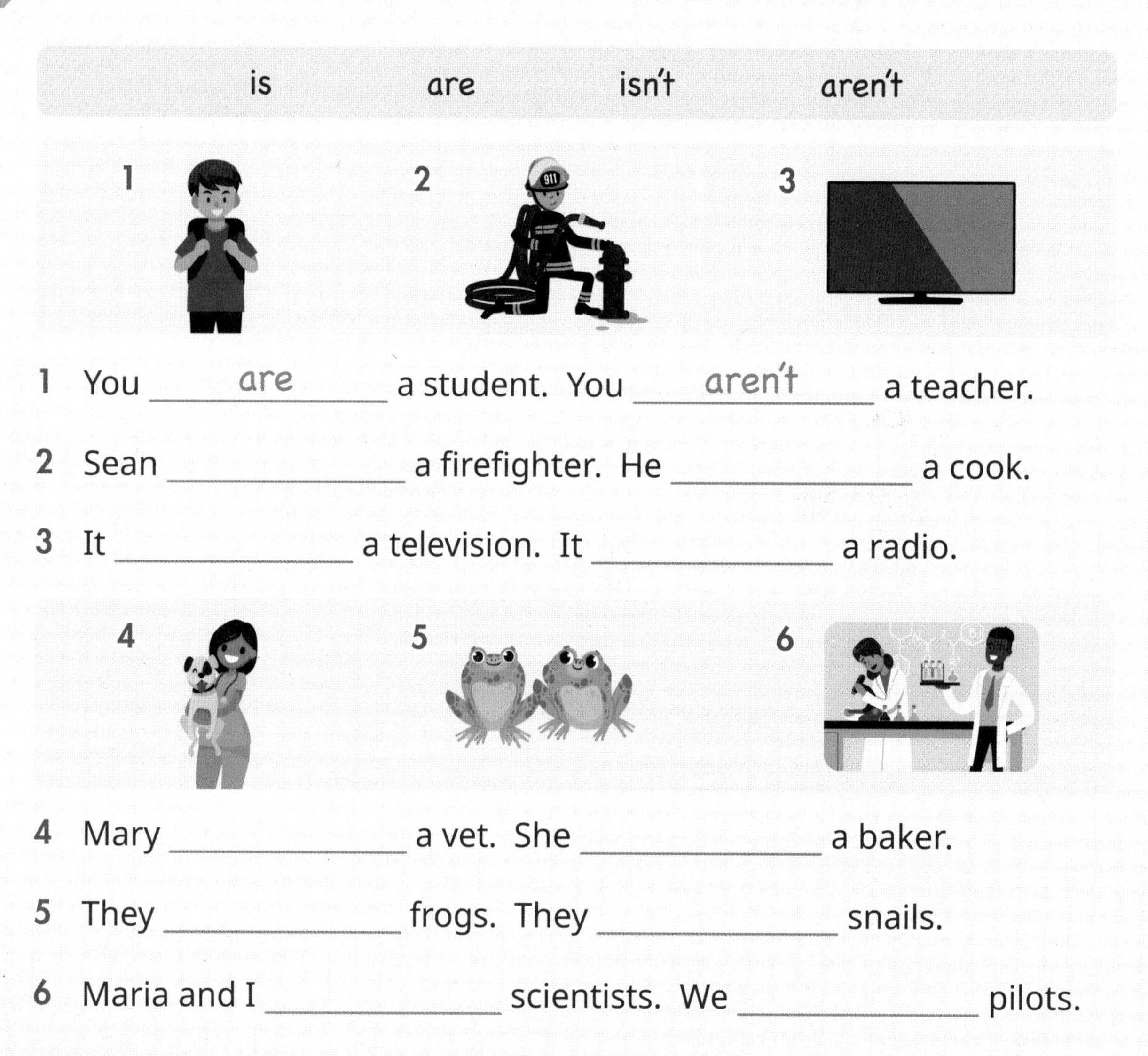

is | are | isn't | aren't

1 You ___are___ a student. You ___aren't___ a teacher.

2 Sean ______ a firefighter. He ______ a cook.

3 It ______ a television. It ______ a radio.

4 Mary ______ a vet. She ______ a baker.

5 They ______ frogs. They ______ snails.

6 Maria and I ______ scientists. We ______ pilots.

Let's Write

What do they do?
Follow the lines and complete the sentences.

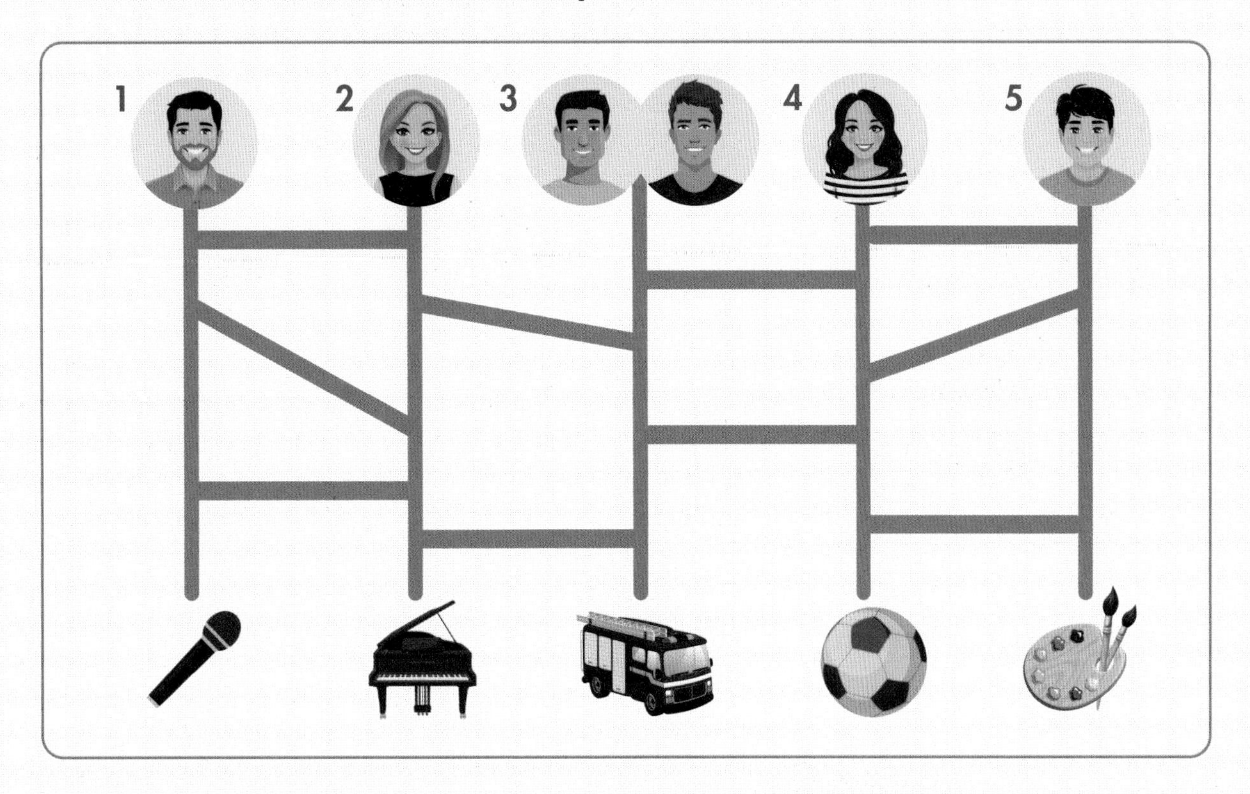

① I'm ___not___ a writer. ___I'm___ a painter.

② You ______ a doctor. ______ a singer.

③ They ______ tennis players. ______ soccer players.

④ She ______ a nurse. ______ a pianist.

⑤ He ______ a police officer. ______ a firefighter.

Be Verb: Questions

Unit 07 Is he tall?

✦ Listen and say.

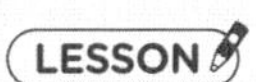

LESSON

1 Be Verb Question: Singular

Question	Answer	
Are you ...?	Yes, I **am**.	No, I**'m not**.
Is he / she / it ...?	Yes, he / she / it **is**.	No, he / she / it **isn't**.

Are you tall?
Yes, I **am**.

Is he strong?
Yes, he **is**.

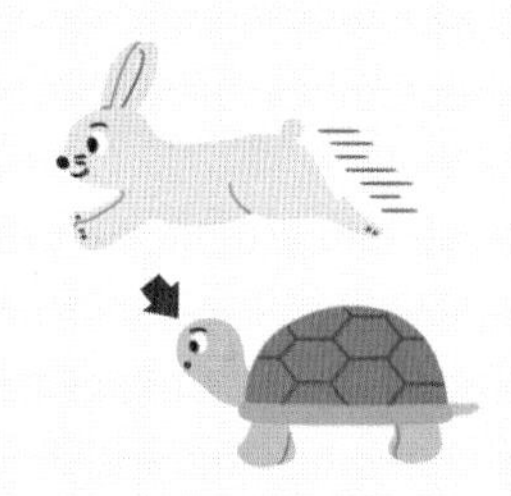

Is it fast?
No, it **isn't**. It's slow.

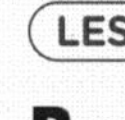

LESSON

2 Be Verb Question: Plural

Question	Answer	
Are you ...?	Yes, we **are**.	No, we **aren't**.
Are we ...?	Yes, you **are**.	No, you **aren't**.
Are they ...?	Yes, they **are**.	No, they **aren't**.

Are you strong?
No, we **aren't**.
We are weak.

Are they young?
Yes, they **are**.

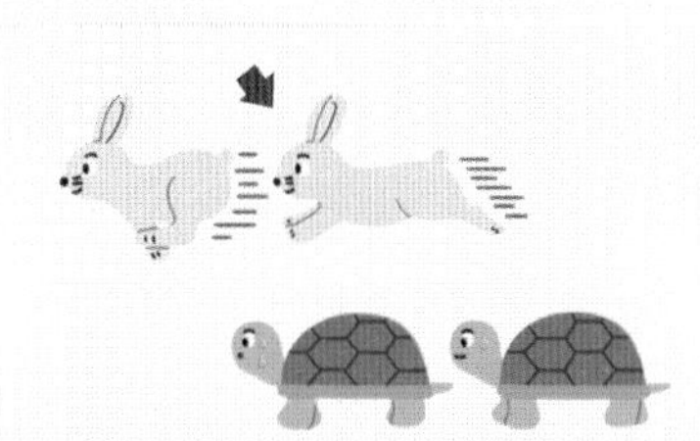

Are they slow?
No, they **aren't**.
They are fast.

Let's Practice

A Look and circle.

① ② ③ ④ ⑤ ⑥

1 Is / Are Tom strong?

2 Is / Are the girls short?

3 Is / Are they weak?

4 Is / Are she old?

5 Is / Are the rabbit fast?

6 Is / Are you sick?

B Look and answer the questions.

①  ②  ③ ④ 

1 Is she a cook? Yes, she is.

2 Are you fast? No, ______ ______.

3 Is the hamster big? No, ______ ______.

4 Are Sam and Lily nurses? Yes, ______ ______.

C Look and write.

1

Are they happy?
Yes, they are.

2

[ ] [ ] strong?
[ ], I [ ].

3

[ ] [ ] young?
[ ], she [ ].

4

[ ] [ ] tall?
[ ], he [ ].

Let's Write

Look and complete the dialogues.

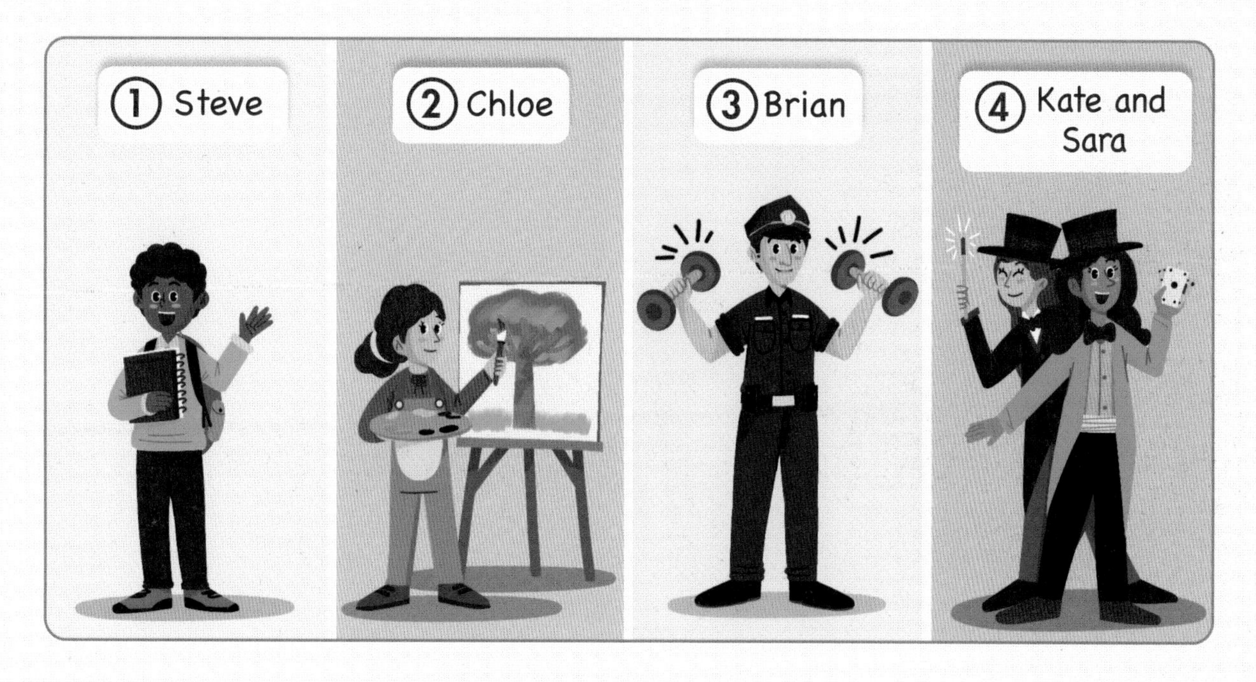

① Q Are you a teacher, Steve?

A No, I'm not. I'm a student.

② Q Is Chloe an artist?

A ________, ________ ________.

Q ________ ________ tall?

A No, she isn't. She's short.

③ Q Is Brian a firefighter?

A ________, ________ ________. He's a police officer.

Q ________ ________ strong?

A Yes, he is.

④ Q Are Kate and Sara singers?

A ________, ________ ________. They're magicians.

Unit 08

There + Be + Noun

There is a bench.

✦ Listen and circle.

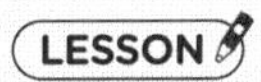

LESSON

1 *There is* + Singular Noun

There is ...	
 **There is** a tree. **There is** an apple.	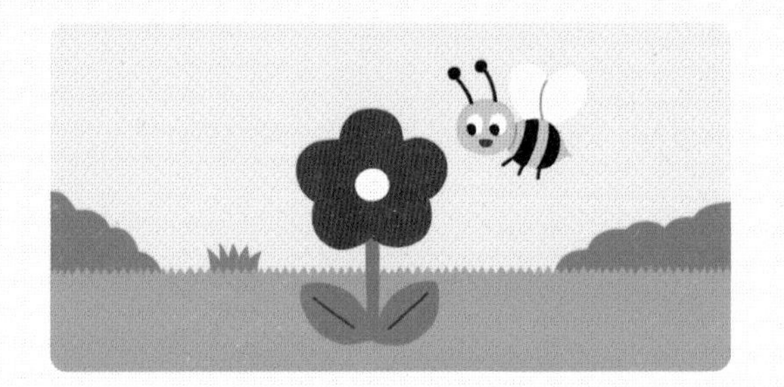 **There is** a flower. **There is** a bee.

LESSON

2 *There* are + Plural Noun

There are ...	
 **There are** trees. **There are** apples.	 **There are** flowers. **There are** bees.

Let's Practice

Look and circle.

1 

There is / are seven roses.

2 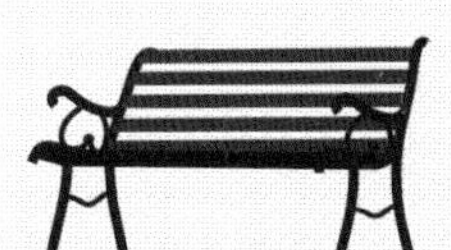

There is / are a bench.

3 

There is / are a bird.

4 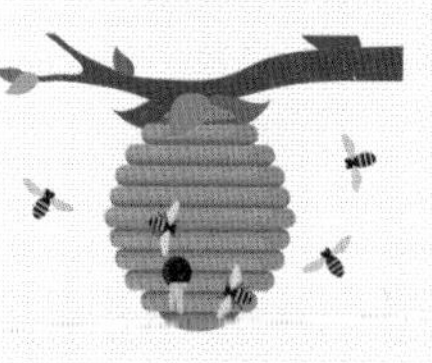

There is / are five bees.

5 

There is / are two tables.

6 

There is / are a lamp.

B Read and write *There is* or *There are*.

1 There is a bicycle.

2 ______ ______ six apples.

3 ______ ______ a flower.

4 ______ ______ a clock.

5 ______ ______ eight candles.

C Circle, choose, and write.

~~trees~~	mice	butterfly
carrot	sheep	peaches

① ② ③ ④ ⑤ ⑥

1 There is / (are) four trees.

2 There is / are a ______.

3 There is / are three ______.

4 There is / are a ______.

5 There is / are two ______.

6 There is / are a ______.

Let's Write

Look, count, and write with *There*.

①	chair	There	are	three	chairs	.
②	table			a		.
③	dish			five		.
④	picture			three		.
⑤	clock			a		.
⑥	child			two		.
⑦	window			a		.

Unit 09

Adjectives

It is a new car.

✦ Listen and circle.

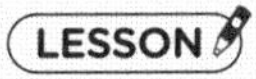

1 Be + *Adjective* / Be + *Adjective* + Noun

Be + Adjective			Be + Adjective + Noun		
The boy	is	**happy**.	He is a	**happy**	boy.
The bag	is	**new**.	It is a	**new**	bag.
The bags	are	**old**.	They are	**old**	bags.

The boy is **happy**. He is a **happy** boy.
The girl is **sad**. She is a **sad** girl.

The car is **new**. It is a **new** car.
The car is **old**. It is an **old** car.

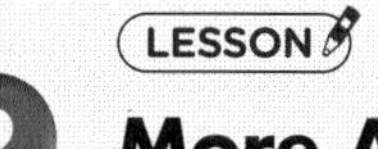

2 More Adjectives

red – yellow	happy ⟷ sad	big ⟷ small	new ⟷ old
blue – green	hungry ⟷ full	long ⟷ short	clean ⟷ dirty
orange – white	angry – sleepy	tall ⟷ short	heavy ⟷ light

Tom is **tall**. He is a **tall** boy.
Sam is **short**. He is a **short** boy.

The basket is **heavy**. It is a **heavy** basket.
The basket is **light**. It is a **light** basket.

The dishes are **clean**. They are **clean** dishes.
The dishes are **dirty**. They are **dirty** dishes.

Let's Practice

A Circle the adjectives.

1 My mom is (angry).

2 It is a long snake.

3 The kid is hungry.

4 It is a new computer.

5 His brothers are tall.

6 The shirts are dirty.

7 They are big elephants.

8 It is a small room.

B Look, choose, and write.

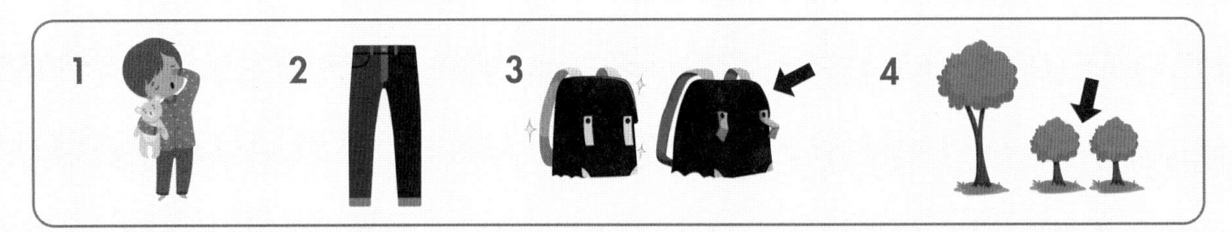

sleepy old short blue

1 The child is sleepy. = He is a sleepy child.

2 The jeans are ______. = They are ______ jeans.

3 The backpack is ______. = It is an ______ backpack.

4 The trees are ______. = They are ______ trees.

C Look, circle, and write.

1

The car is dirty / clean.

= It is a dirty car.

2

The apples are red / green.

= They are ______ ______.

3

The baby is happy / sad.

= She is a ______ ______.

4

The box is heavy / light.

= It is a ______ ______.

Let's Write

Look, choose, and complete the sentences.

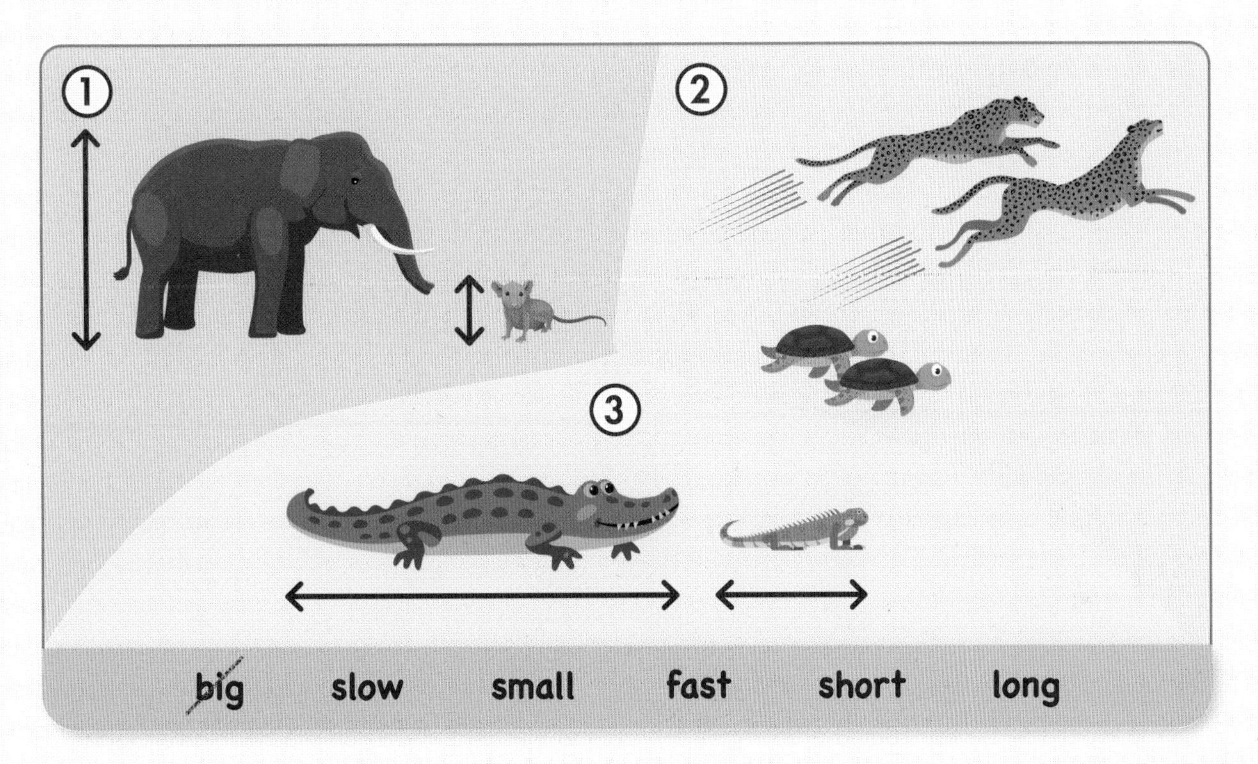

① The elephant is big.

It is a big elephant.

The mouse is ______.

It is a ______ ______.

② The cheetahs are ______.

They are ______ ______.

The turtles are ______.

They are ______ ______.

③ The alligator is ______.

It is a ______ ______.

The iguana is ______.

It is a ______ ______.

Unit 10

Review 2

Unit 06-09

A Read and circle.

1 She am / are / is a dancer.

2 I am / are / is happy.

3 There is / are a window.

4 The boys isn't / aren't short.

5 There is / are three chairs.

6 There is / are five oranges.

7 The rabbit isn't / aren't slow.

8 We am / are / is painters.

B Look, choose, and write.

old black heavy hungry

1 The shoes are old.

They are old shoes.

2 The girl is __________.

She is a __________ __________.

3 The box is __________.

It is a __________ __________.

4 The cats are __________.

They are __________ __________.

C Circle, choose, and write.

a cook	a magician	tables	a bench	scientists

1 She is / are a cook.

2 Sally and Ted is / are ______________.

3 There is / are ______________.

4 There is / are ______________.

5 The man is / are ______________.

D Read and complete the dialogues.

1
Q Are they pilots?
A Yes, they are.

2
Q ______ ______ sleepy?
A No, I'm not.

3
Q ______ the dishes clean?
A No, ______ ______.

4
Q ______ Tom a writer?
A Yes, ______ ______.

5
Q ______ the pencil long?
A Yes, ______ ______.

6
Q ______ the girl sad?
A No, ______ ______.

Mini Test 1

◆ Unit 01-09 ◆

◆ **Check the correct sentences.**

1 ☐ This are my boots.
☐ These are my boots.

2 ☐ We have a cheese.
☐ We have cheese.

3 ☐ There is a tomato.
☐ There are a tomato.

4 ☐ The man isn't a pianist.
☐ The man aren't a pianist.

5 ☐ It's an ant. An ant is small.
☐ It's an ant. The ant is small.

6 ☐ This is Tom jacket.
☐ This is Tom's jacket.

◆ **Look and write.**

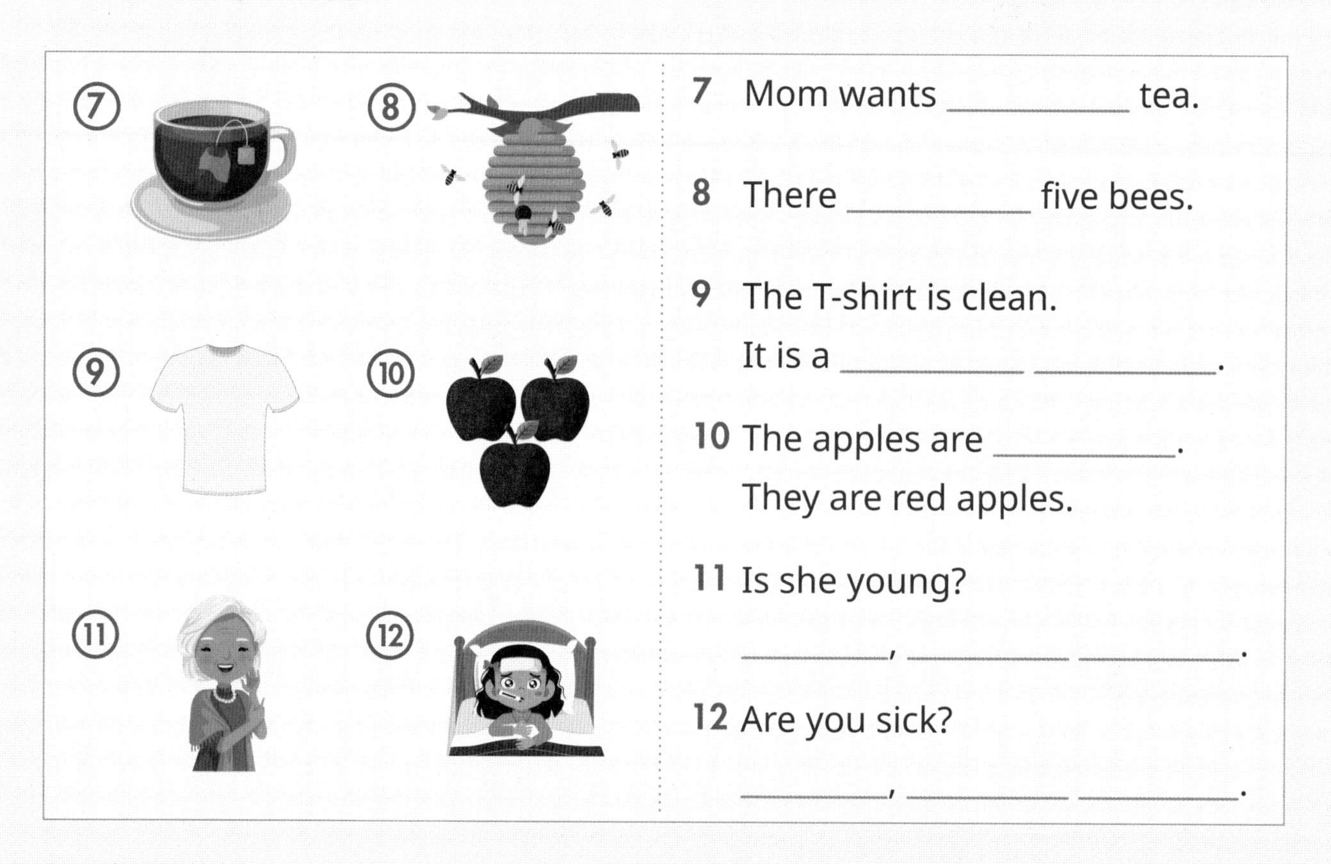

7 Mom wants __________ tea.

8 There __________ five bees.

9 The T-shirt is clean.
It is a __________ __________.

10 The apples are __________.
They are red apples.

11 Is she young?
__________, __________ __________.

12 Are you sick?
__________, __________ __________.

◆ Change the underlined words.

13 The man <u>is</u> strong. **Negative** → The man ________ strong.

14 <u>I'm not</u> a nurse. **Positive** → ________ ________ a nurse.

15 I see <u>a fox</u>. **Plural (two)** → I see ________ ________.

16 I see <u>three mice</u>. **Singular** → I see ________ ________.

◆ Find and correct the mistakes.

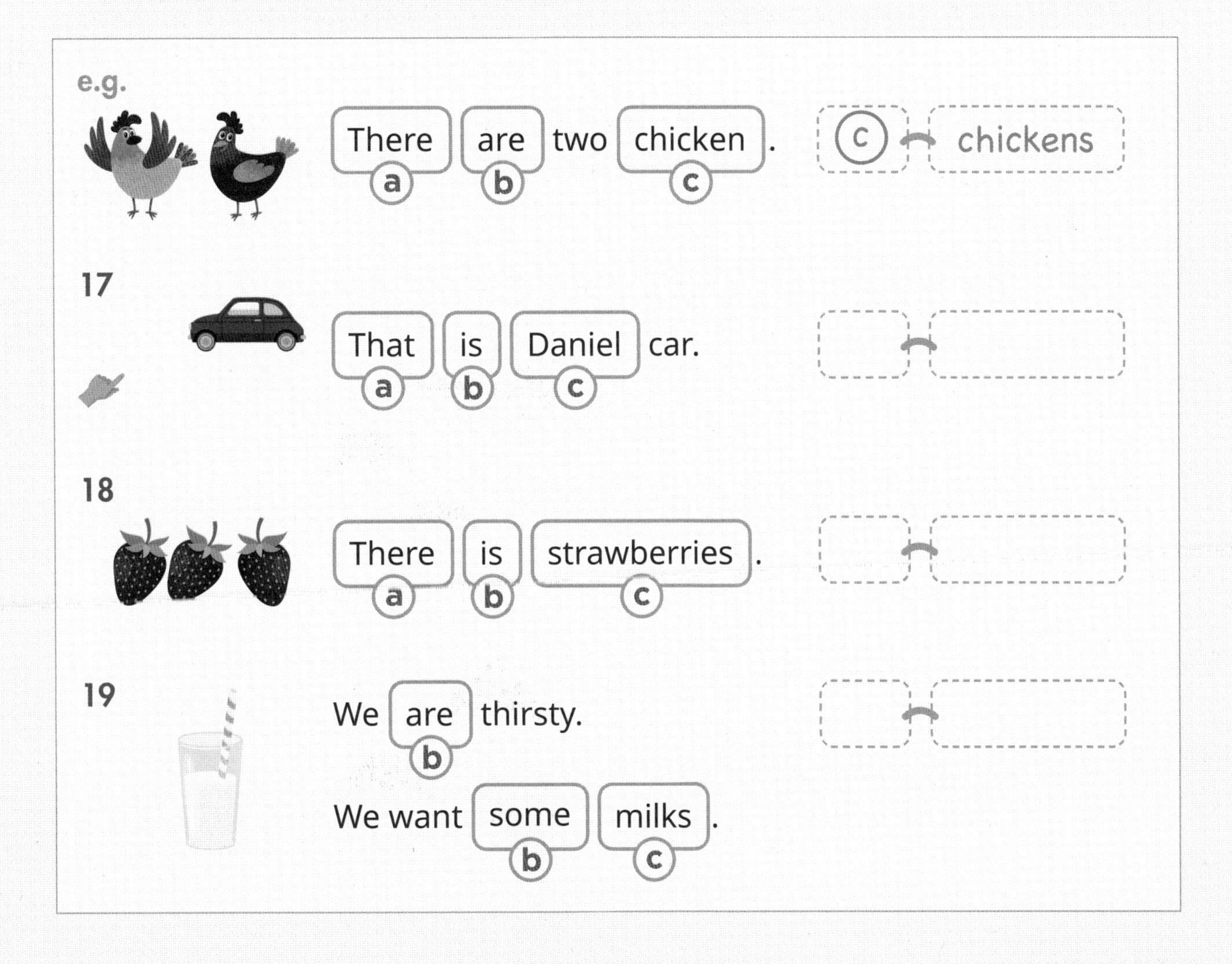

Present Simple: Positives

Unit 11 Tom has breakfast.

✦ Listen and circle.

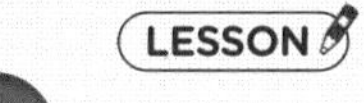

1 Present Simple

Subject	Verb (-s / -es / -ies)
I You We They	sleep. go. cry.
He She It	sleep**s**. go**es**. cr**ies**.

They **sleep**.
They **cry**.

She **sleeps**.
She **cries**.

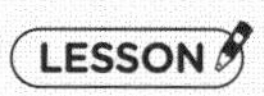

Regular and Irregular Verbs

Regular Verbs			Irregular Verbs
-s	-es	-ies	
read - read**s** sleep - sleep**s** drink - drink**s**	wash - wash**es** teach - teach**es** kiss - kiss**es** fix - fix**es** go - go**es**	cry - cr**ies** study - stud**ies** fly - fl**ies**	have - **has**
play - play**s**			

I **wash** my face every day.
He **washes** his face every day.

I **have** breakfast every day.
He **has** breakfast every day.

They **go** to school at 8:00.
Sue **goes** to school at 8:30.

They **study** English at 2:00.
Sue **studies** math at 2:00.

Let's Practice

Read and circle.

1 I go / goes to school at 8:00.

2 A bird fly / flies in the sky.

3 She watch / watches TV.

4 Tom eat / eats lunch at 1:00.

5 He teach / teaches English.

6 They sleep / sleeps at 9:00.

B Look and write.

1 have → I have breakfast every day.

2 read → My dad __________ a newspaper every day.

3 study → He __________ math every day.

4 play → My sister and I __________ games at 5:00.

5 cook → My mom __________ dinner every day.

6 go → Claire __________ to bed at 10:00.

C What does your family do every day? Choose and write.

~~go to school~~	drink coffee	wash the dishes
study English	watch TV	read a book

In the morning,

1 I go to school.

2 My mom __________

3 My dad __________

At night,

4 I __________

5 My mom __________

6 My dad __________

Let's Write

What do they do? Look and complete the sentences.

①	read	I read a book.
②	watch	Dad ________ TV.
③	cry	And he ________ .
④	do	Mom ________ the dishes.
⑤	help	My sister ________ Mom.
⑥	fix	My brother ________ the toy car.

Present Simple: Negatives

Unit 12 They don't drink milk.

✦ Listen and circle.

At 12:00, Lily has a hamburger.
Ben doesn't have a hamburger.
He has soup.

Lily and Ben drink juice.
They don't drink milk.
They don't like milk.

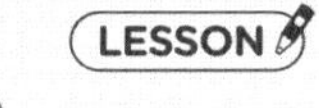

1 Present Simple: Don't

Subject	Don't	Verb
I	don't	**drink.** **eat.** **cry.**
You		
We		
They		

don't = do not

I **don't drink** milk.
I drink juice.

We **don't eat** salads.
We eat hamburgers.

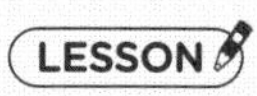

2 Present Simple: Doesn't

Subject	Doesn't	Verb
He	doesn't	drink.
She		eat.
It		cry.

doesn't = does not

Ben **doesn't study** Chinese.
He studies English.

Kate **doesn't make** cookies.
She makes a cake.

It **doesn't have** arms.
It has wings.

Let's Practice

A Look and circle.

1 I don't / doesn't drink juice. I drink water.

2 She don't / doesn't play the piano. She plays the guitar.

3 The kids don't / doesn't eat salads. They eat pizza.

4 The baby don't / doesn't cry. He smiles.

B Read and write *don't* or *doesn't*.

1 She doesn't like vegetables.

2 Spiders ______ have wings.

3 My brother ______ do his homework.

4 Sam and I ______ play soccer.

5 My uncle ______ drive a car.

C Look and write the correct forms of the verbs.

① go ② make ③ study ④ eat

1 We ___go___ to school.
We ___don't___ ___go___ to work.

2 She ______ cookies.
She ______ ______ a cake.

3 The students ______ French.
They ______ ______ English.

4 The koala ______ leaves.
It ______ ______ meat.

Let's Write

Lia and I are twins. Look and complete the sentences.

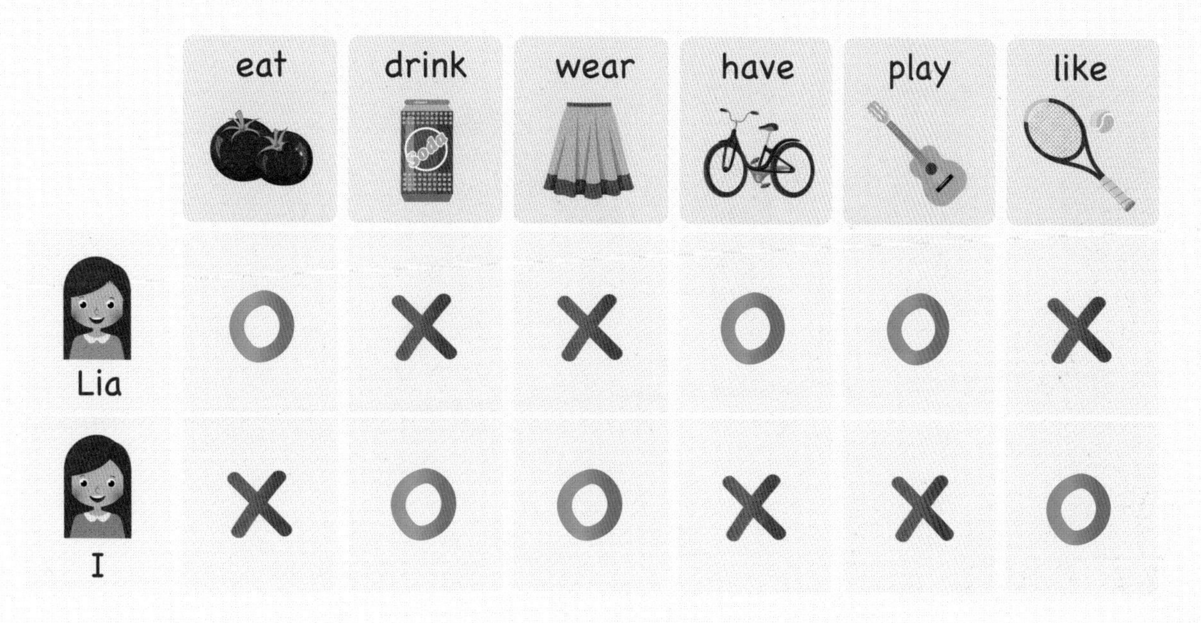

① Lia eats tomatoes. I don't eat tomatoes.

② I drink soda. Lia ______ ______ soda.

③ I wear skirts. Lia ______ ______ skirts.

④ Lia has a bike. I ______ ______ a bike.

⑤ Lia plays the guitar. I ______ ______ the guitar.

⑥ I like tennis. Lia ______ ______ tennis.

Present Simple: Questions

Unit 13 Does he play soccer?

✦ Listen and circle.

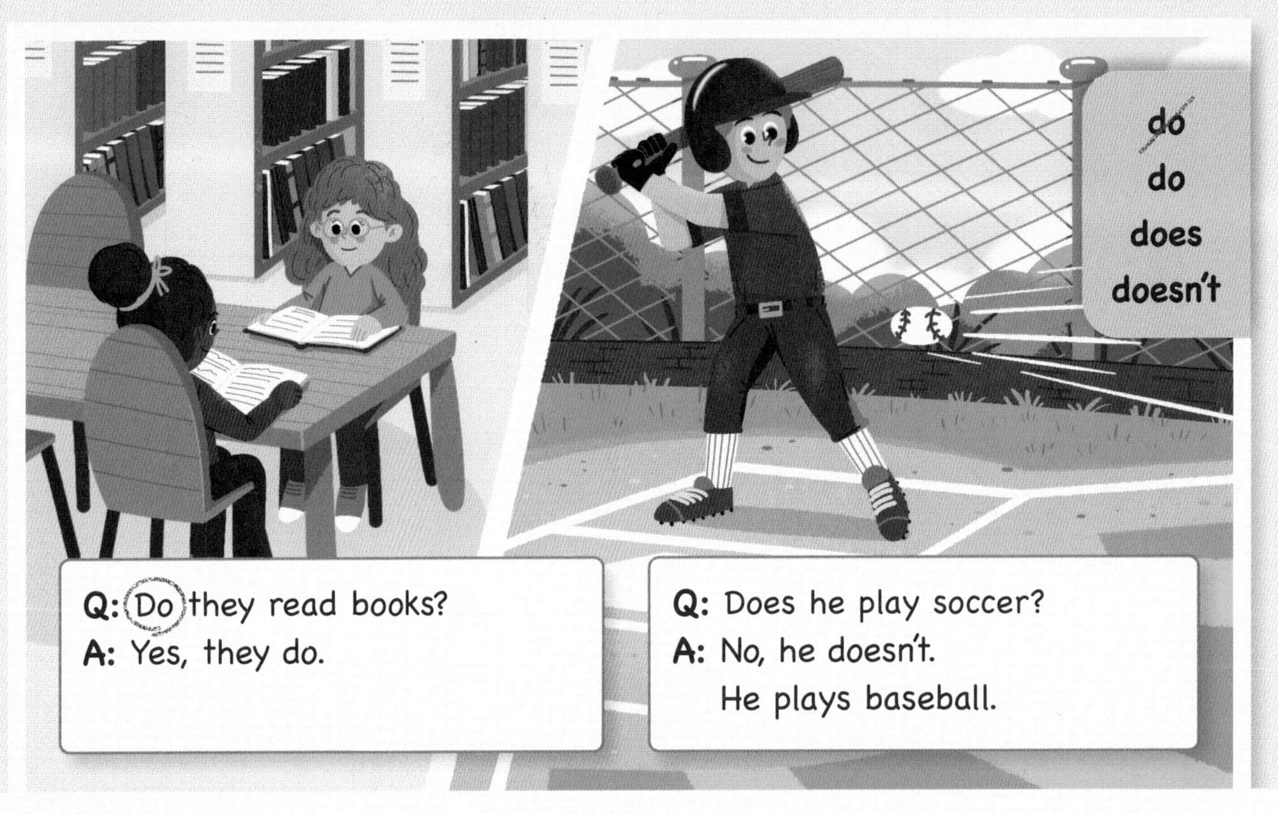

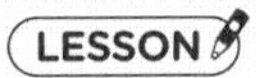

LESSON

1 Present Simple: Do you/we/they ...?

Question			Answer	
Do	you	**sing**?	Yes, I / we **do**.	No, I / we **don't**.
	we		Yes, you **do**.	No, you **don't**.
	they		Yes, they **do**.	No, they **don't**.

Do you **play** soccer?
Yes, I **do**.

Do they **sing**?
No, they **don't**. They dance.

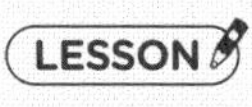

Present Simple: Does he/she/it ...?

Question			Answer	
Does	he	**sing**?	Yes, he **does**.	No, he **doesn't**.
	she		Yes, she **does**.	No, she **doesn't**.
	it		Yes, it **does**.	No, it **doesn't**.

Does he **swim**?
Yes, he **does**.

Does she **draw** a picture?
No, she **doesn't**.
She reads a book.

Does the bird **sing**?
Yes, it **does**.

Let's Practice

A Circle and write.

1 (Do) / Does you [play] soccer? — play

2 Do / Does he [ ] a cat? — have

3 Do / Does penguins [ ]? — swim

4 Do / Does they [ ] books? — read

5 Do / Does Sue [ ] her homework? — do

B Look and answer the questions.

① ②  ③  ④ 

1 Does she help her mom? Yes, she does.

2 Do they walk to school? No, ______ ______.

3 Does the boy dance? No, ______ ______.

4 Do you paint a picture? Yes, ______ ______.

C Look and write.

Every Day	06:00 AM get up at 6	Milk drink milk	have breakfast	exercise
Bell	X	X	O	O
Andy	O	O	O	X
Susie	O	O	X	X

1 [Does] Bell get up at 6? [No], she [doesn't].

2 [ ] Andy drink milk? [ ], he [ ].

3 [ ] Bell and Andy have breakfast? [ ], they [ ].

4 [ ] Andy and Susie exercise? [ ], they [ ].

Let's Write

What do you do every day? Write O or × about yourself.

Every Day	play the piano	go swimming	watch TV	read a book
Max	O	×	×	O
Ann	O	×	O	O
Mary	×	O	O	×
You				

Look at the activity above. Then, complete the dialogues.

① Does Max play the piano? Yes, he does.

② ______ Ann go swimming? ______, ______ ______.

③ ______ Mary watch TV? ______, ______ ______.

④ ______ Max and Ann read a book? ______, ______ ______.

⑤ ______ you play the piano? ______, ______ ______.

⑥ ______ you read a book? ______, ______ ______.

Unit 14

Review 3

Unit 11-13

A Check the correct sentences.

1
- [x] We study English every day.
- [ ] We studies English every day.

2
- [ ] Luke play computer games.
- [ ] Luke plays computer games.

3
- [ ] My brother and I don't watch TV.
- [ ] My brother and I doesn't watch TV.

4
- [ ] Do you go to school every day?
- [ ] Does you go to school every day?

B Look and write.

1 I ___sleep___ at 10:00 every day.

2 She ________ ________ the violin. She plays the guitar.

3 We ________ water every day.

4 They ________ ________ hamburgers. They eat pizza.

5 The plane ________ in the sky.

C Look and complete the dialogues.

1 listen

Do they listen to music?

Yes, they do.

2 play

__________ you __________ basketball?

No, __________ __________.

3 make

__________ Sally __________ a cake?

No, __________ __________.

4 have

__________ a penguin __________ wings?

Yes, __________ __________.

D Correct the mistakes.

1 She doesn't eats carrots. → eat

2 Danny have a brother. →

3 They doesn't study French. →

4 Ms. Steven teachs English. →

5 Do your dad read a book every day? →

Mini Test 2

✦ Unit 06-13 ✦

◆ Read and circle.

1 They am / are / is actors.

2 The box isn't / aren't heavy.

3 He do / does the dishes.

4 Lucy am / are / is a firefighter.

5 Is / Are the giraffes tall?

6 I don't / doesn't have a pet.

7 We watch / watches a movie.

8 Do / Does Mike get up early?

◆ Look and write.

⑨ 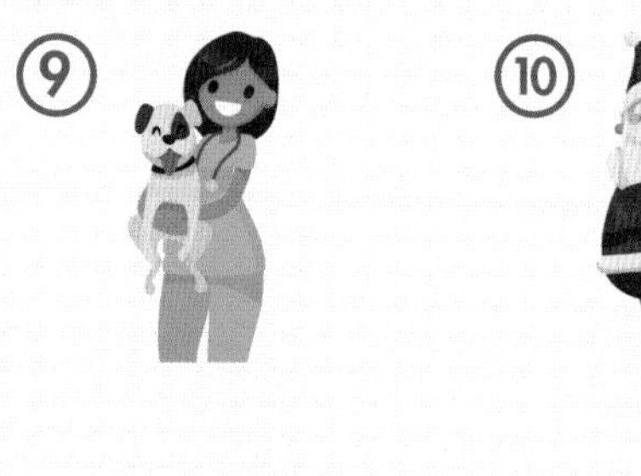

⑩ 

⑪ 

⑫ 

⑬ 

⑭ 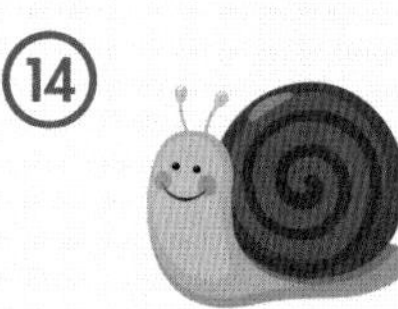

9 She __________ a vet.

10 He has a big bag.

It is a __________ bag.

11 There __________ seven roses.

12 Are the jeans blue?

Yes, __________ __________.

13 Does your dad drive a car?

Yes, __________ __________.

14 Does a snail have legs?

No, __________ __________.

Choose and complete the sentences.

fly isn't is aren't kisses	15 Look! There ____________ a bench. 16 Mom ____________ the baby every day. 17 Sam and I ____________ hungry. We're full. 18 The children ____________ the kites. 19 She ____________ a nurse. She's a doctor.

Find and correct the mistakes.

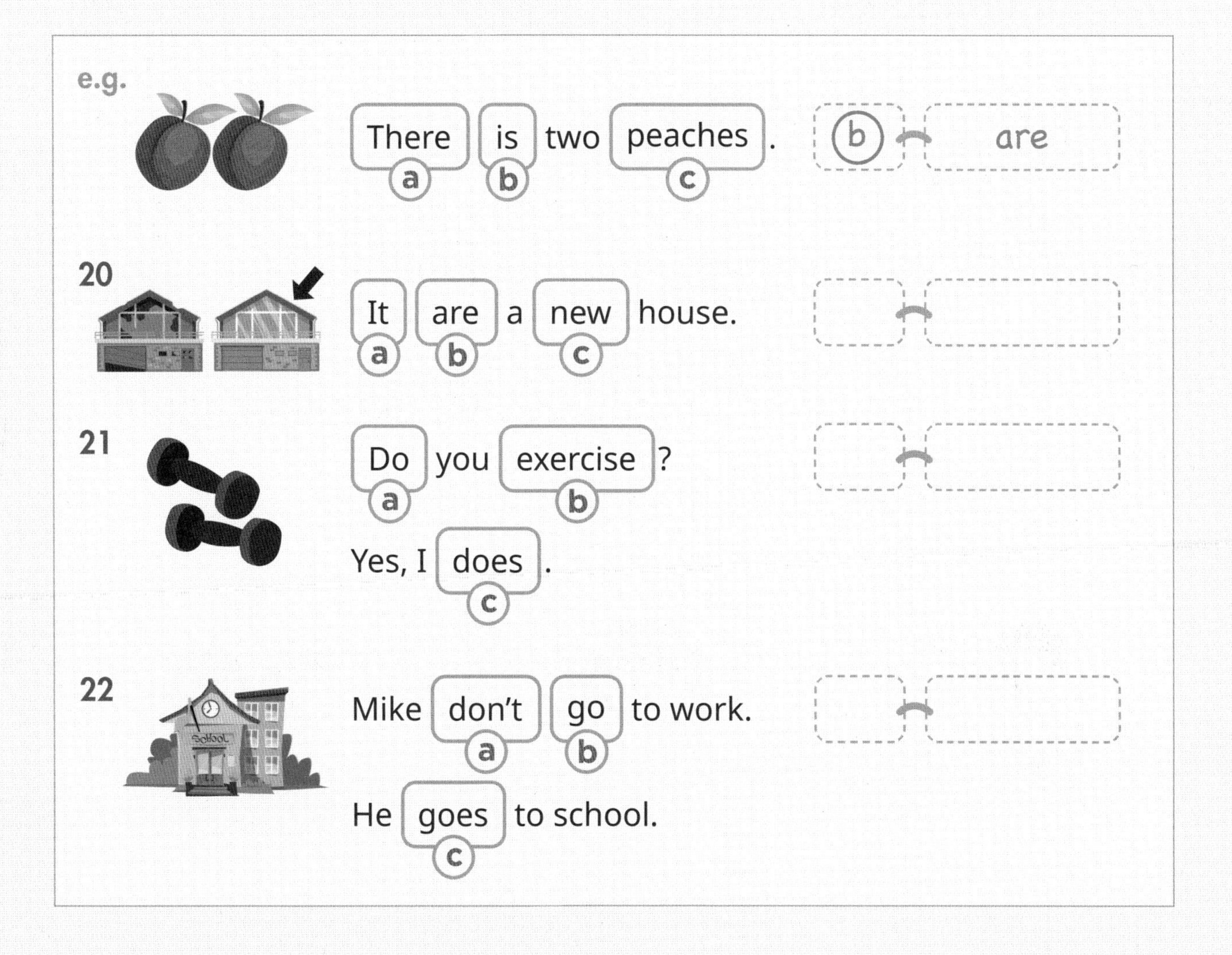

Present Continuous: Positives

Unit 15 The girl is dancing.

✦ Listen and circle.

LESSON

 Present Continuous

Subject	Be	Verb-ing
I	**am**	
He / She / It	**is**	sing**ing**.
We / You / They	**are**	

I **am singing**.

She **is eating**.

They **are sleeping**.

2 Verb + -ing

+ -ing	-e + -ing	-double consonant + -ing
sing - sing**ing**	dance - danc**ing**	sit - sit**ting**
eat - eat**ing**	ride - rid**ing**	run - run**ning**
read - read**ing**	write - writ**ing**	swim - swim**ming**

Tom **is jumping**.

Mina **is riding** a horse.

The dog **is running**.

Tom and Sally **are reading**.

The girls **are dancing**.

The ducks **are swimming**.

Let's Practice

A Write the -ing forms of the verbs.

1 read … reading

2 sit …

3 dance …

4 run …

5 write …

6 sing …

B Look, circle, and write.

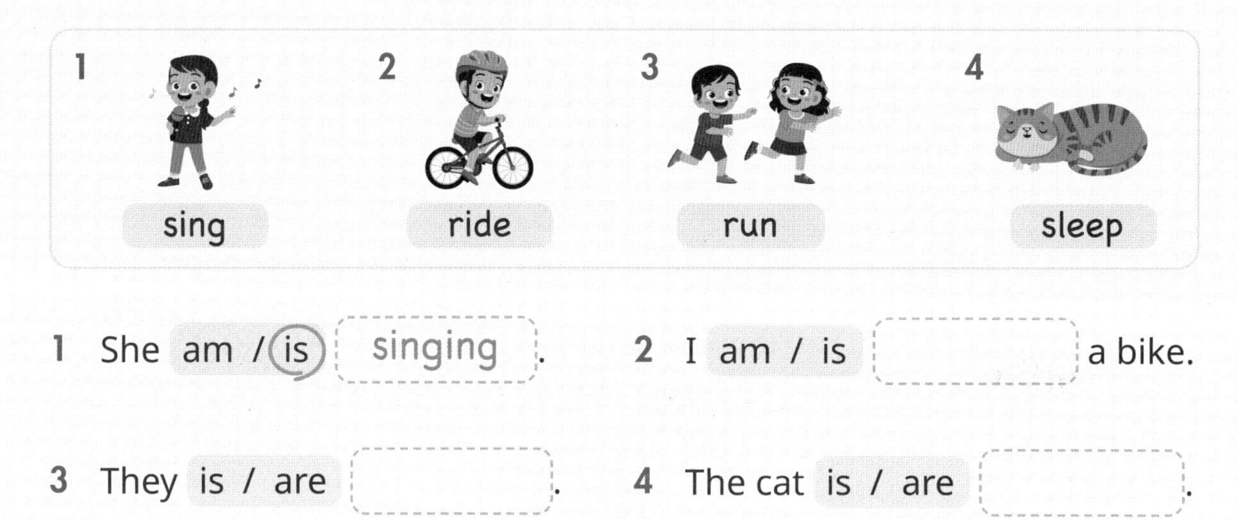

1 She am / (is) [singing]. 2 I am / is [ ] a bike.

3 They is / are [ ]. 4 The cat is / are [ ].

C Look and write.

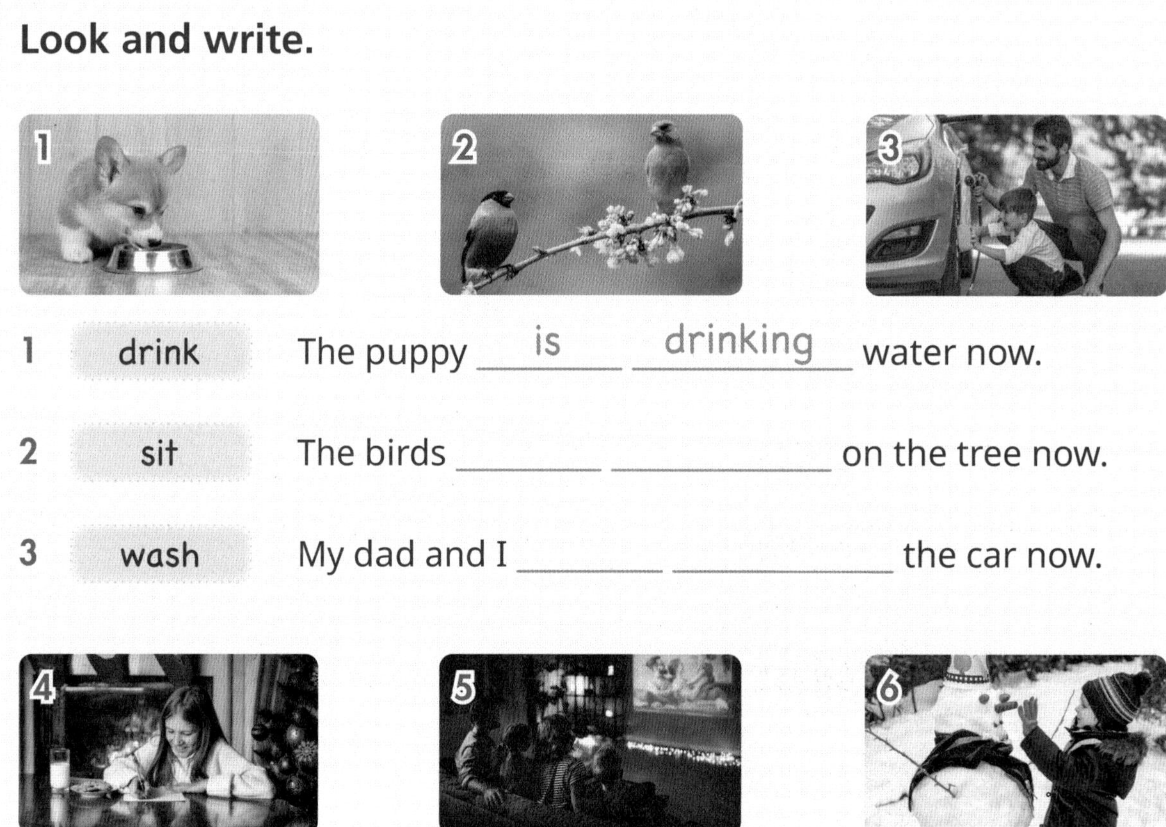

1 drink — The puppy __is__ __drinking__ water now.

2 sit — The birds ________ ____________ on the tree now.

3 wash — My dad and I ________ ____________ the car now.

4 write — I ________ ____________ a letter now.

5 watch — They ________ ____________ a movie now.

6 make — The boy ________ ____________ a snowman now.

Let's Write

Look and complete the sentences.

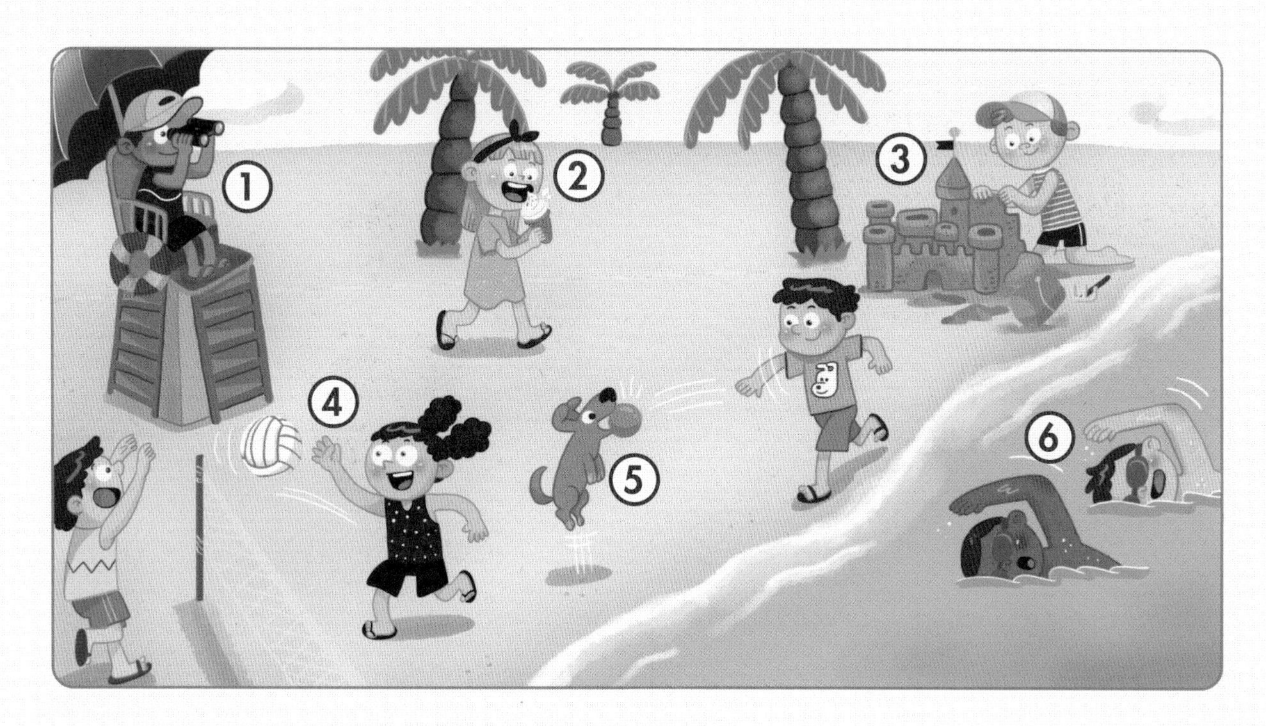

Many people are at the beach now.

①	watch	I	am	watching	people.
②	eat	The girl			ice cream.
③	make	The boy			a sandcastle.
④	play	The children			volleyball.
⑤	catch	The dog			a ball.
⑥	swim	The men			.

Present Continuous: Negatives

Unit 16 The woman isn't sitting.

✦ Listen and circle.

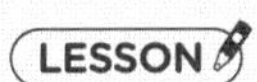

1 Present Continuous with *Not*

Subject	Be	Not	Verb-ing
I	**am**		
He / She / It	**is**	**not**	eat**ing**.
We / You / They	**are**		

I **am not eating**.
I am cooking.

She **is not writing**.
She is drawing.

They **are not running**.
They are walking.

LESSON 2 Short forms

Subject	Be + Not	Verb-ing
I	**am not** (= **I'm not**)	
He / She / It	**is not** (= **isn't**)	eat**ing**.
We / You / They	**are not** (= **aren't**)	

I'm not studying.
I'm listening to music.

The cat **isn't playing**.
It is sleeping.

They **aren't standing**.
They are sitting.

Let's Practice

A Look and circle.

① 

② 

③  

④ 

1 She is / isn't cooking now. She is washing the dishes.

2 They are / aren't listening to music now.

3 My sister isn't / aren't studying now. She is watching TV.

4 She and I am not / aren't standing now. We are sitting.

B Look and write.

1 walk 2 write 3 study 4 make

1 The horse isn't walking now. It is running.

2 He ______ ______ now. He is reading a book.

3 They ______ ______ now. They are playing basketball.

4 We ______ ______ a snowman now.
We are making a sandcastle.

C Look and write the correct forms of the verbs.

1
read — We are reading books.
play — We aren't playing in the library.

2
draw — The girl ______ ______ a picture.
write — She ______ ______ in a diary.

3
eat — It ______ ______ a banana.
drink — It ______ ______ water.

4
sit — They ______ ______ on the chairs.
stand — They ______ ______.

Let's Write

Look and complete the sentences.

① Amy ___is___ jumping now.

She ___isn't___ ___sitting___.
[sit]

② Luke and Ben ______ running now.

They ______ ______.
[walk]

③ Bell ______ listening to music now.

She ______ ______ a song.
[sing]

④ Mr. Brown ______ drinking some water now.

He ______ ______ a picture.
[take]

Present Continuous: Questions

Are you reading?

Listen and say.

LESSON

1 Present Continuous: How to make a question

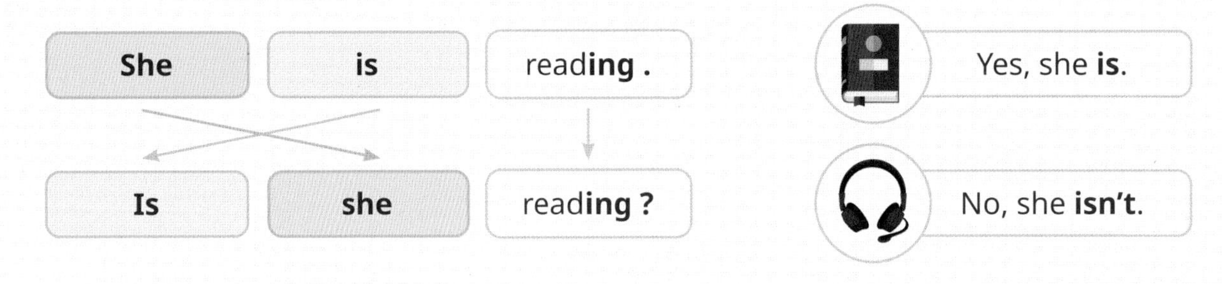

LESSON

2 Present Continuous Question: Singular

Question			Answer	
Are	you	eating?	Yes, I **am**.	No, I**'m not**.
Is	he / she / it		Yes, he / she / it **is**.	No, he / she / it **isn't**.

Are you **reading**?
Yes, I **am**.

Is she **studying**?
No, she **isn't**.

Is the pig **drinking**?
Yes, it **is**.

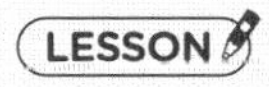

3 Present Continuous Question: Plural

Question			Answer	
Are	you	eat**ing**?	Yes, we **are**.	No, we **aren't**.
	they		Yes, they **are**.	No, they **aren't**.

Are you **riding** bikes?
Yes, we **are**.

Are they **cleaning**?
Yes, they **are**.

Are the pigs **eating**?
No, they **aren't**.

Let's Practice

A Write the questions with the verbs.

1. drink — ___Is___ he ___drinking___ milk now?
2. cut — ______ you ______ the paper now?
3. cry — ______ the baby ______ now?
4. write — ______ Sofia ______ a letter now?

B Look and answer the questions.

1 2 3 4

1 Is Tina skating? No, she isn't.

2 Is he playing the violin? Yes, ______ ______.

3 Are you flying kites? Yes, ______ ______.

4 Are they riding bikes? No, ______ ______.

C Look and write.

① 
laugh

② 
brush

③ 
make

1 Are they laughing? Yes, they are.

2 ______ Ben ______ his teeth? No, ______ ______.

3 ______ you ______ a cake? Yes, ______ ______.

④ 
clean

⑤ 
swim

⑥ 
draw

4 ______ your sister ______? Yes, ______ ______.

5 ______ the frog ______? No, ______ ______.

6 ______ they ______ pictures? Yes, ______ ______.

Let's Write

Look and complete the dialogues.

① Q ___Are___ you ___washing___ the dog? [wash]

A Yes, ___I___ ___am___.

② Q ________ your dad ________ the grass? [cut]

A Yes, ________ ________.

③ Q ________ the butterflies ________? [fly]

A No, ________ ________. They are sitting on the flowers.

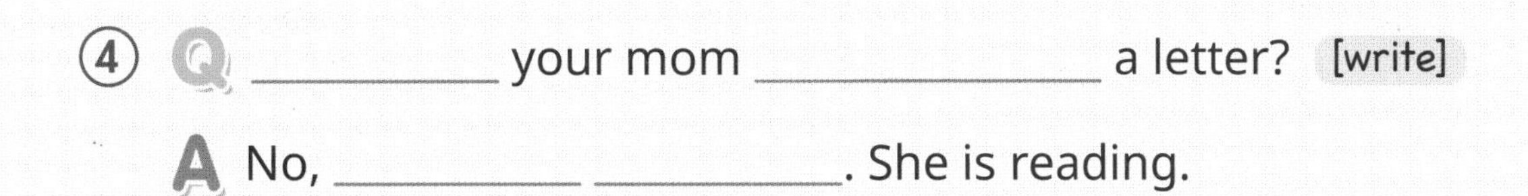

④ Q ________ your mom ________ a letter? [write]

A No, ________ ________. She is reading.

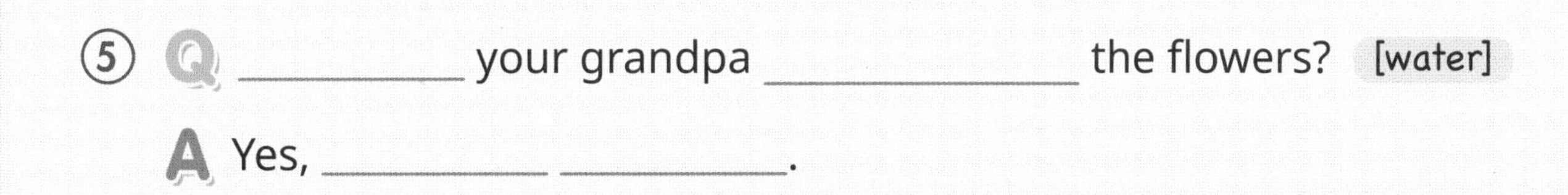

⑤ Q ________ your grandpa ________ the flowers? [water]

A Yes, ________ ________.

Unit 18

Review 4

Unit 15-17

A Check the correct sentences.

1
- [ ] She is writeing an email.
- [x] She is writing an email.

2
- [ ] We isn't singing now.
- [ ] We aren't singing now.

3
- [ ] Are the men siting now?
- [ ] Are the men sitting now?

4
- [ ] Is your mom work now?
- [ ] Is your mom working now?

B Look and write.

wash

run

③

study

1 Minho __is__ __washing__ his face now.

2 The boy ________ ________ now.

3 I ________ ________ ________ now. I'm listening to music.

④

make

drink

⑥

play

4 The kids ________ ________ a sandcastle now.

5 Sarah ________ ________ juice now. She's drinking milk.

6 We ________ ________ baseball now. We're playing basketball.

C Look, write, and circle.

1 [Is] she cooking now? — Yes, she is. / (No, she isn't.)

2 [ ] you riding a bike now? — Yes, I am. / No, I'm not.

3 [ ] the cat sleeping now? — Yes, it is. / No, it isn't.

4 [ ] they standing now? — Yes, they are. / No, they aren't.

D Look and complete the dialogues.

1

Are you watching TV now? [watch]

Yes, I am.

2

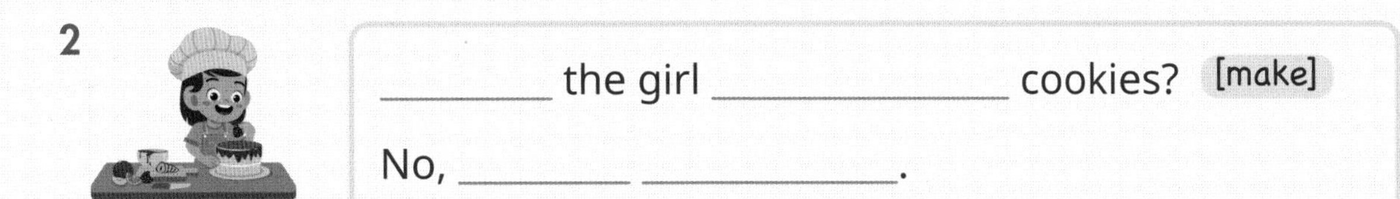

______ the girl ______ cookies? [make]

No, ______ ______.

3

______ the frog ______ on the leaf? [sit]

Yes, ______ ______.

4

______ you ______ now? [swim]

Yes, ______ ______.

Mini Test 3

Read and circle.

1 We are plays / playing tennis.

2 He has / haves lunch at 1:00.

3 We don't / doesn't like fruits.

4 The dog isn't / aren't eating.

5 Is / Does a turtle have a tail?

6 I'm takeing / taking a shower.

Look and write the correct forms of the verbs.

⑦ dance ⑧ study ⑨ walk ⑩ cry ⑪ help

7 They ___________ ________________ now.

8 Harry ________________ English every day.

9 The horse ___________ ________________ now. It is running.

10 ___________ the kids ________________ now?
No, they aren't.

11 ___________ you ________________ your mom every day?
Yes, I do.

◆ **Change and rewrite the sentences.**

12 The boy is skating. Negative → ______________________.

13 She brushes her teeth. Question → ______________________?

14 Noah and I fly a kite. Negative → ______________________.

15 They are taking pictures. Question → ______________________?

◆ **Find and correct the mistakes.**

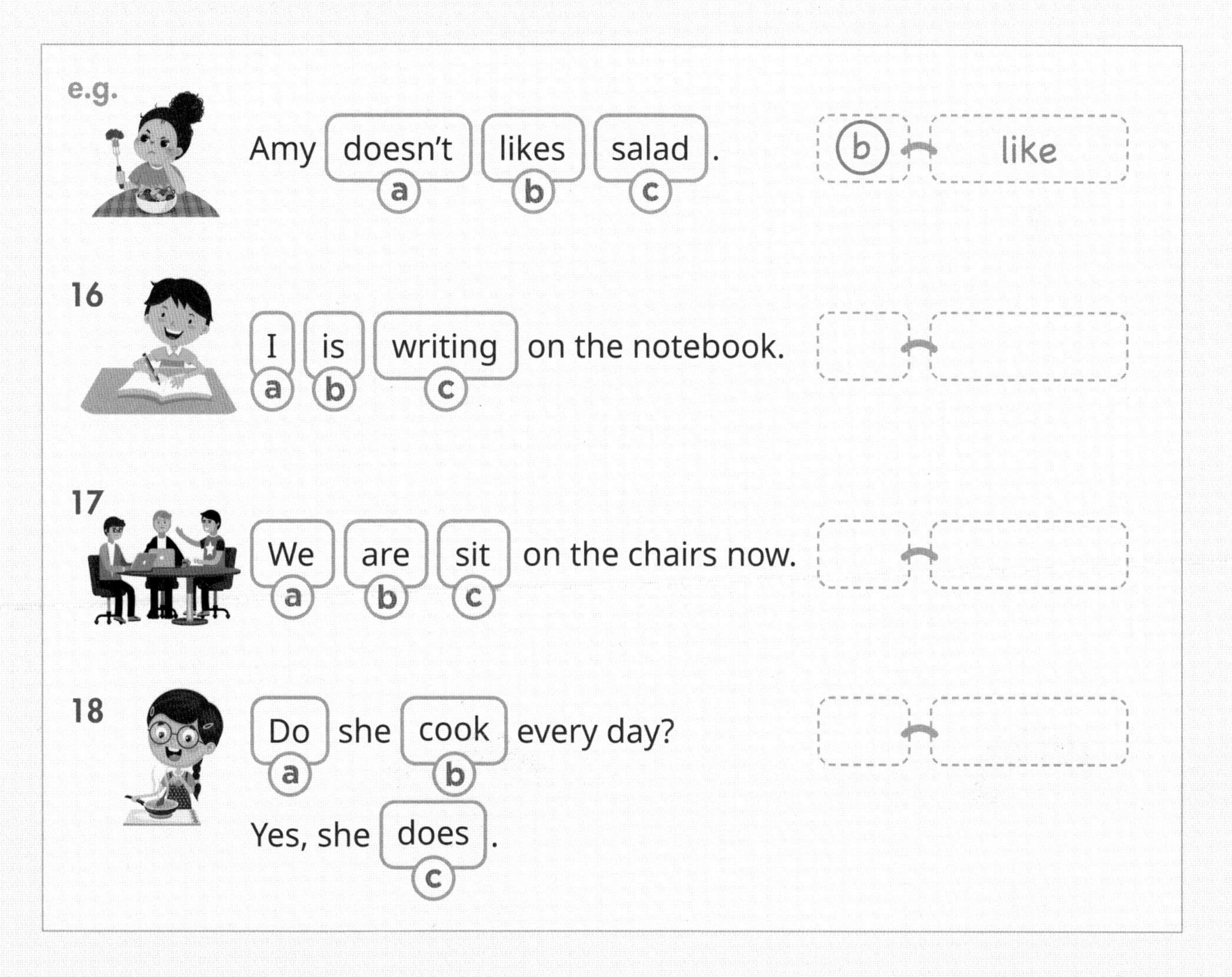

Unit 19

Modal Verb: Can / May

May I take a picture?

Listen and circle.

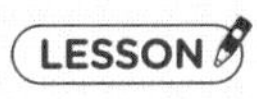

1 Can: Ability

Can	
I / He / They **can** swim.	
I / He / They **can't** swim.	
Can you swim? Yes, I / we **can**. No, I / we **can't**.	**Can** he swim? Yes, he **can**. No, he **can't**.

A: I **can** cook.
Can you cook?
B: Yes, I **can**.

A: She **can** skate.
Can he skate?
B: No, he **can't**.

LESSON

Can / May: Permission

Can	May
You / She / They **can** go in.	You / She / They **may** go in.
You / She / They **can't** go in.	You / She / They **may not** go in.
Can I / we go in? Yes, you **can**. No, you **can't**.	**May** I / we go in? Yes, you **may**. No, you **may not**.

Can I have an apple?
Yes, you **can**.

May I use your phone?
No, you **may not**.

You **can't** watch TV.

Let's Practice

Read and write with *can* or *can't*.

1 fly — Horses don't have wings. They can't fly.

2 bake — Anna is a baker. She ________ ________ cookies.

3 drive — The boy is too young. He ________ ________ a car.

4 speak — She teaches Chinese. She ________ ________ Chinese.

5 jump — A kangaroo has long legs. It ________ ________ high.

B Look and write *may* or *may not*.

1 You ___may not___ run here.

2 You ______________ come in now.

3 You ______________ watch TV now.

4 You ______________ take a picture here.

C Look and write.

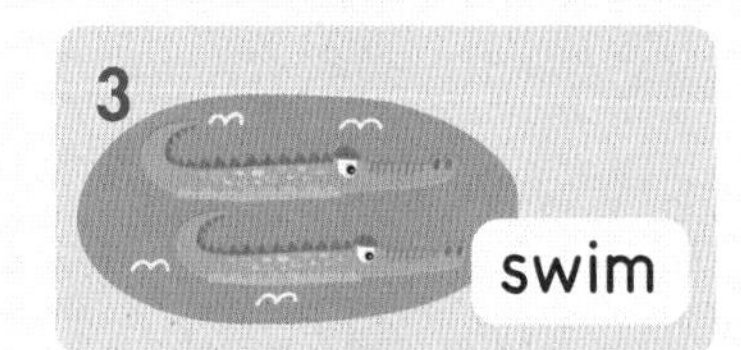

1 Can you [skate]? [Yes], I [can].

2 Can she [ ] a bike? [ ], she [ ].

3 Can alligators [ ]? [ ], they [ ].

4 May I [ ] the computer? [ ], you [ ] [ ].

5 May I [ ] your pen? [ ], you [ ].

6 Can I [ ] this painting? [ ], you [ ].

Let's Write

Look and complete the dialogues.

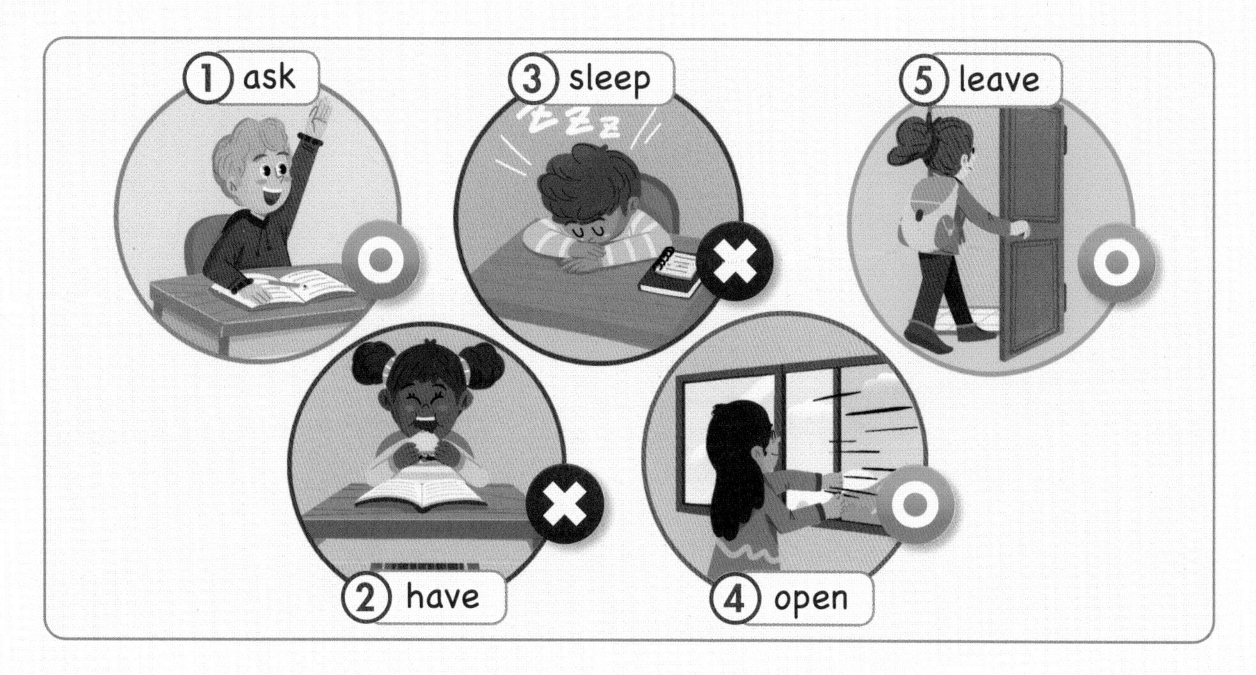

① Q May I ___ask___ a question in class?

A ___Yes___, ___you___ ___may___.

② Q May I ________ a sandwich in class?

A ________, ________ ________ ________.

③ Q Can I ________ in class?

A ________, ________ ________.

④ Q Can I ________ the window?

A ________, ________ ________.

⑤ Q May I ________ the classroom?

A ________, ________ ________.

Unit 20 Whose jacket is it?

✦ Listen and circle.

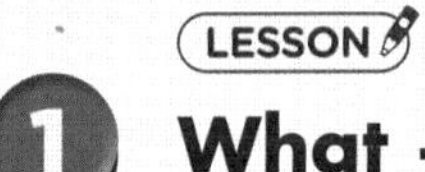

1 What + be ...?

Things, Animals, and Places	
Q: **What** is it? A: It is **a backpack**.	Q: **What** are they? A: They are **puppies**.

What is it?
It is **a coat**.

What are they?
They are **boots**.

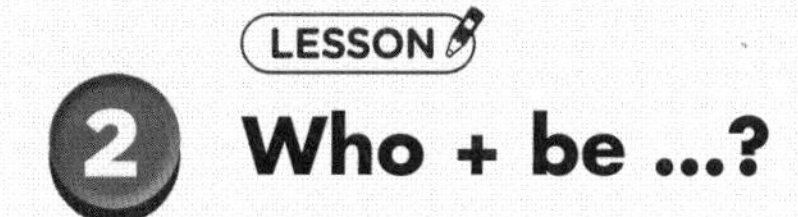

2 Who + be ...?

People	
Q: Who is he? **A:** He is **Adam's brother**.	**Q: Who** are you? **A:** I am **Kate's friend**. We are **Kate's friends**.
Q: Who is she? **A:** She is **Lina's sister**.	**Q: Who** are they? **A:** They are **my parents**.

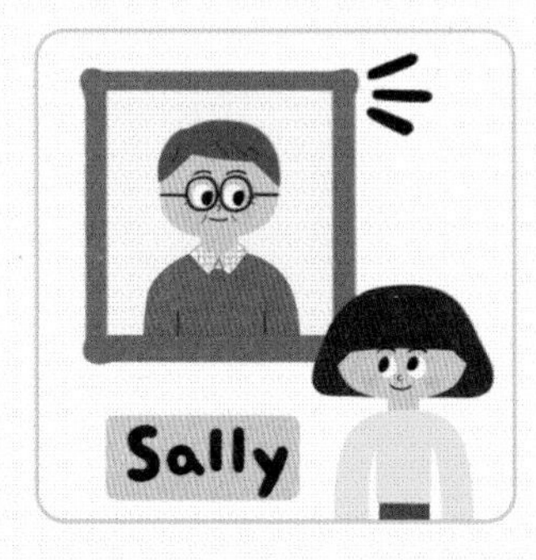

Who is he?
He is **Sally's grandfather**.

Who are they?
They are **Brian's parents**.

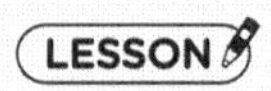

3 Whose + *Noun* + be ...?

Possessions	
Q: Whose *jacket* is it? **A:** It is **Andy's jacket**.	**Q: Whose** *shoes* are they? **A:** They are **Kate's shoes**.

Whose *coat* is it?
It is **Clara's coat**.

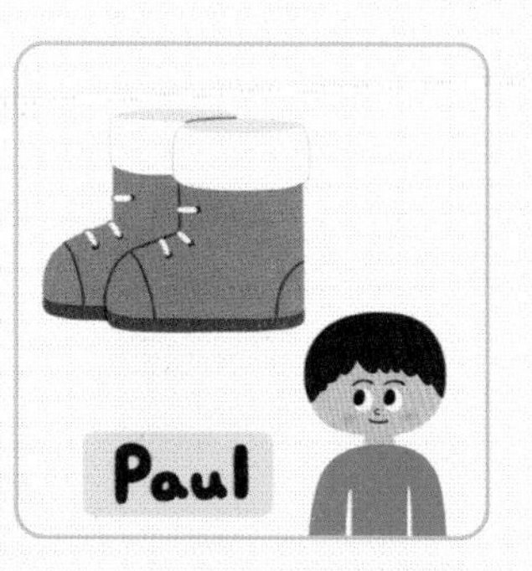

Whose *boots* are they?
They are **Paul's boots**.

Let's Practice

Circle, write, and check.

①  ②  ③ 

1 Who / What is it?
- [x] It is a shirt.
- [ ] They are shirts.

2 Who / Whose shoes ______ they?
- [ ] It is Amy's shoe.
- [ ] They are Amy's shoes.

3 Who / What ______ you?
- [ ] I am Tom's brother.
- [ ] We are Tom's brothers.

B Look and write.

① 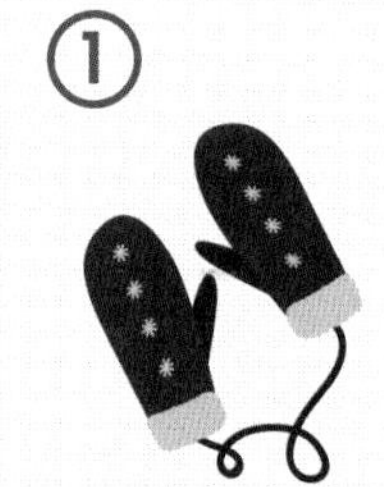 ② 

③ ④

1 Whose mittens are they?
They are Bella's mittens.

2 ______ ______ she?
______ ______ my grandmother.

3 ______ ______ they?
______ ______ boots.

4 ______ ______ ______ it?
______ ______ Eric's jacket.

Let's Write

Look and complete the dialogues.

① Who are they ?

They are Luke and Clara.

② ______ ______ ______ ?

It is a pencil case.

③ ______ ______ ______ ______ ?

They are Luke's gloves.

④ ______ ______ ______ ______ ?

It is Clara's mirror.

⑤ ______ ______ ______ ?

They are pencils.

Prepositions of Time

It is at 1 o'clock.

Listen and circle.

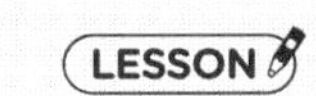

1 *at, on,* and *in*

at + time	on + day on + date	in + month
at 2 o'clock	**on** Tuesday **on** May 1st	**in** July

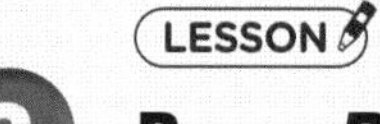

2 Be + *Preposition* + Noun

When is the game?
It is **at** 2 o'clock.

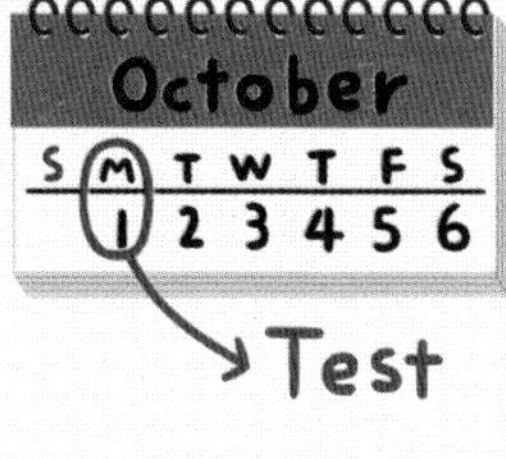

When is the test?
It is **on** Monday.

When is your birthday?
It is **in** April.

When is the movie?
It is **at** 7:30.

When is the party?
It is **on** June 10th.

When is Christmas?
It is **in** December.

Let's Practice

A Look and match.

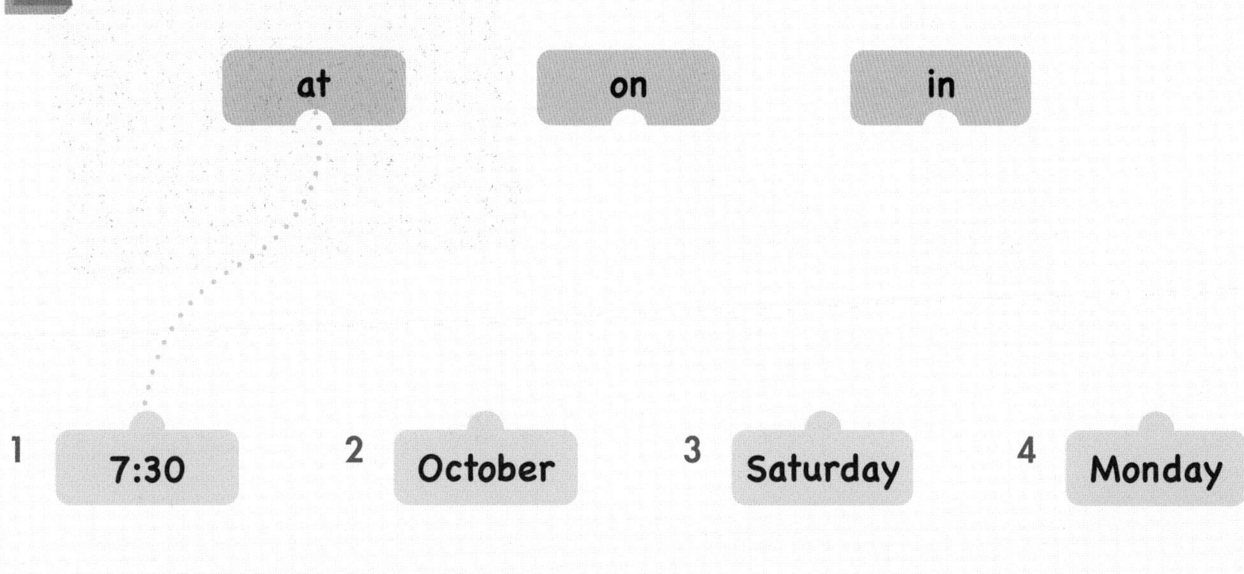

B Read and write *at, on,* or *in.*

1 I get up [at] 7 o'clock.

2 We have dinner [ ] 6:30.

3 He plays soccer [ ] Friday.

4 Christmas is [ ] December.

5 Lucy has a test [ ] April 5th.

6 Mom's birthday is [ ] November.

C Look and write *at, on,* or *in.*

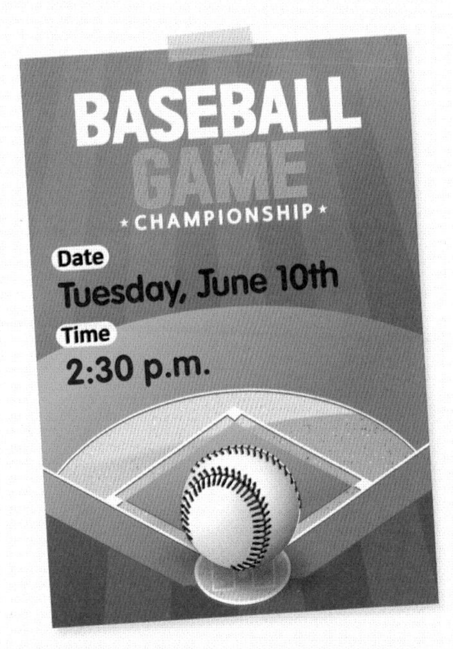

When is the baseball game?

1 It's ___in___ June.

2 It's ________ Tuesday.

3 It's ________ 2:30.

When is the Halloween party?

4 It's ________ October 31st.

5 It's ________ Saturday.

6 It's ________ 7 o'clock.

Let's Write

This is Eric's schedule. Look and complete the sentences.

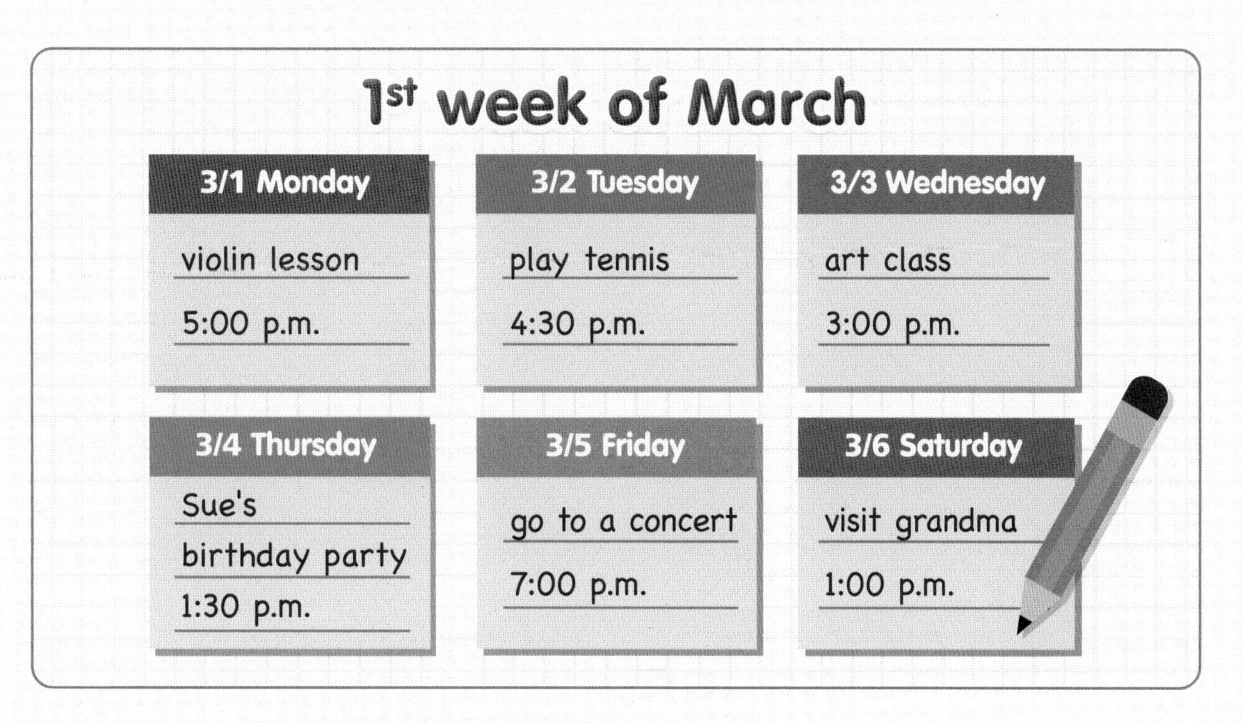

① Eric has a violin lesson on Monday. [day]

② He has art class ______ ______. [day]

③ Sue's birthday party is ______ March. [month]

④ The party is ______ March 4th. [date]

⑤ It starts ______ ______. [time]

⑥ Eric goes to a concert ______ 7:00 ______ Friday. [time] [day]

Unit 22

Review 5

Unit 19-21

A Read and circle.

1 They have a test at / in 5 o'clock.

2 You not may / may not talk in class.

3 The school picnic is in / on Friday.

4 The dolphin can jump / jumps high.

5 The soccer game is on / in March.

6 Q Who / What is she? A She is Noah's sister.

7 Q What are they? A It is / They are socks.

B Read and match.

1 Can your aunt drive a car?

2 May I use your camera?

3 What is it?

4 When is your birthday?

5 Whose gloves are they?

They are Paul's gloves.

No, she can't.

It is on August 5th.

Yes, you may.

It is a coat.

C Look and write.

1 Who is the boy?

He is my brother.

2 When is the dinner?

7:30 p.m.

It is ______ 7:30.

3 Can I touch this painting?

No, ______ ______.

4 ______ ______ they?

They are mittens.

5 When is the art class?

Tuesday

It is ______ Tuesday.

D Correct the mistakes.

1 A cat can catches a mouse. → catch

2 The summer vacation is on August. →

3 **Q** Who notebooks are they? →

A They are Amy's notebooks.

4 **Q** May I play outside? →

A No, you can't.

Mini Test 4

Read and circle.

1 I am / are helping my mom.

2 My birthday is in / on May 4th.

3 The party is at / on Sunday.

4 A cheetah is runing / running .

5 Who / What is the man?

6 Who / Whose book is it?

7 My mom and I isn't / aren't cooking.

8 He isn't washes / washing the car.

Look and write.

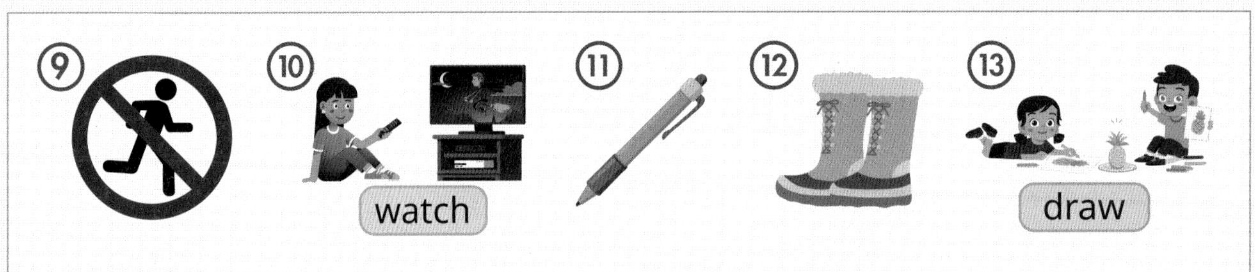

9 You ____________ ____________ run in here.

10 Susan ____________ ____________ TV now.

11 Can I borrow your pen? Yes, ____________ ____________.

12 ____________ ____________ they? They are boots.

13 ____________ they ____________ now? Yes, they are.

◆ **Choose and complete the sentences.**

in	can't	may	carrying	at

14 The movie starts ____________ 3 o'clock.

15 Halloween is ____________ October.

16 ____________ I ask a question now?

17 My brother is sick. He ____________ go to school.

18 The woman is ____________ some boxes now.

◆ **Find and correct the mistakes.**

e.g. The puppy [aren't](a) [playing](b). It [is](c) sleeping. — (a) → isn't[is not]

19 [Who](a) glasses [are](b) they? [They](c) are my dad's glasses. — ( ) → ____________

20 May I [open](a) the window? Yes, [you](b) [can](c). — ( ) → ____________

21 [Is](a) [your sister](b) [cleans](c) the house now? — ( ) → ____________

Grammar Audio Lessons

- If you need help to understand the grammar, scan the QR code using your phone.
- This will give you immediate access to detailed audio lessons in Korean.
- You can select and play each lesson from the list.

Unit	❶	❷
Unit 01	a/an + Noun	the + Noun
Unit 02	Plural Nouns: -s and -es	Plural Nouns: -ies, -ves, and others
Unit 03	Count and Non-count Nouns	a/an/some + Noun
Unit 04	Demonstratives	Possessives
Unit 06	Be Verb: Singular	Be Verb: Plural
Unit 07	Be Verb Question: Singular	Be Verb Question: Plural
Unit 08	There is + Singular Noun	There are + Plural Noun
Unit 09	Be + Adjective / Be + Adjective + Noun	More Adjectives
Unit 11	Present Simple	Regular and Irregular Verbs

Unit 12
1. Present Simple: Don't
2. Present Simple: Doesn't

Unit 13
1. Present Simple: Do you/we/they ...?
2. Present Simple: Does he/she/it ...?

Unit 15
1. Present Continuous
2. Verb + -ing

Unit 16
1. Present Continuous with Not
2. Short forms

Unit 17
1. Present Continuous: How to make a question
2. Present Continuous Question: Singular
3. Present Continuous Question: Plural

Unit 19
1. Can: Ability
2. Can / May: Permission

Unit 20
1. What + be ...?
2. Who + be ...?
3. Whose + Noun + be ...?

Unit 21
1. at, on, and in
2. Be + Preposition + Noun

Scope & Sequence

Unit	Grammar Point	Key Sentences	Key Vocabulary
01	**Nouns and Articles (a/an/the)**	It is a pencil. The pencil is long. Look at the sky.	a pencil, the pencil, an eraser, the easer, the sun, the moon, the sky, the sea
02	**Plural Noun:** -s, -es, -ies, -ves, others	They are chickens. They are puppies. They are mice.	chickens, trees, peaches, brushes, glasses, boxes, babies, puppies, wolves, knives, feet, men, children, mice
03	**Count and Non-count Nouns**	I want an egg. I want cookies. I want some juice.	egg, cookie, orange, peach, bread, cheese, juice, water
04	**Demonstratives and Possessives**	This is my watch. These are his gloves. That is Sue's scarf.	watch, gloves, scarf, gift, pet, car
05	**Review 1**		
06	**Be Verb:** **Positives and Negatives**	She is a singer. She isn't a pianist.	singer, pianist, painter, writer, magician, actor
07	**Be Verb: Questions**	Are you tall? Is she old? Is he strong?	tall, young, old, strong, weak, fast, slow
08	**There + Be + Noun**	There is a tree. There are flowers.	a tree, an apple, a flower, a bee, a bench, trees, apples, flowers, bees
09	**Adjectives**	The car is new. It is a new car. The boy is happy. He is a happy boy.	red, yellow, blue, happy, sad, hungry, full, angry, sleepy, big, small, long, tall, short, new, old, clean, dirty, heavy, light
10	**Review 2 + Mini Test 1 (Unit 01-09)**		

Unit	Grammar Point	Key Sentences	Key Vocabulary
11	**Present Simple: Positives**	I wash my face every day. He has breakfast every day. Sue goes to school at 8:30.	read, sleep, drink, play, wash, teach, kiss, fix, go, cry, study, fly, have
12	**Present Simple: Negatives**	I don't drink milk. He doesn't have a hamburger.	drink, eat, study, make, cry, have, like
13	**Present Simple: Questions**	Do you play soccer? Does he swim?	read, draw, play, sing, dance, swim
14	**Review 3 + Mini Test 2 (Unit 06-13)**		
15	**Present Continuous: Positives**	I am singing. Mina is riding a horse. The ducks are swimming.	eating, sleeping, reading, jumping, playing, singing, dancing, writing, riding, sitting, swimming, running
16	**Present Continuous: Negatives**	I'm not studying. She isn't writing. They aren't running.	cooking, eating, watching, drawing, writing, walking, running, playing, listening, studying, sleeping, sitting, standing
17	**Present Continuous: Questions**	Are you reading? Is she studying? Are they cleaning?	eating, drinking, studying, reading, drawing, cleaning, cutting, riding
18	**Review 4 + Mini Test 3 (Unit 11-17)**		
19	**Modal Verb:** Can for Ability, Can and May for Permission	She can skate. Can he swim? Can I have an apple? May I use your phone?	swim, skate, cook, go, take, have, use, touch, watch
20	**Wh- Question:** What, Who, Whose	What is it? Who are they? Whose coat is it?	jacket, coat, backpack, shoes, boots, parent, grandfather, brother, sister, friend
21	**Prepositions of Time:** at, on, in	It is at 2 o'clock. It is on Monday. It is on June 10th. It is in April.	1 o'clock, 7:30, Monday, Tuesday, Sunday, June 6th, May 1st, April, July, December
22	**Review 5 + Mini Test 4 (Unit 15-21)**		

Spiral Syllabus

Oh! My Grammar 1		Oh! My Grammar 2		Oh! My Grammar 3	
U01	Nouns and Articles (a/an)	U01	Nouns and Articles (a/an/the)	U01	Nouns and Articles (a/an/the)
U02	Plural Nouns	U02	Plural Nouns	U02	Present Simple: Be Verbs
U03	Subject Pronouns	U03	Count and Non-count Nouns	U03	There + Be + Noun
U04	Review 1	U04	Demonstratives and Possessives	U04	Review 1
U05	Be Verb: Positives	U05	Review 1	U05	Present Simple: Positives and Negatives
U06	Be Verb: Negatives	U06	Be Verb: Positives and Negatives	U06	Present Simple: Questions
U07	Be Verb: Questions	U07	Be Verb: Questions	U07	Present Continuous: Positives and Negatives
U08	Review 2	U08	There + Be + Noun	U08	Present Continuous: Questions
U09	Demonstrative Pronouns	U09	Adjectives	U09	Review 2
U10	Demonstrative Pronoun: Questions	U10	Review 2	U10	Let's and Imperatives
U11	Possessive Adjectives	U11	Present Simple: Positives	U11	Future: Positives and Negatives
U12	Review 3	U12	Present Simple: Negatives	U12	Future: Questions
U13	Present Simple: Positives	U13	Present Simple: Questions	U13	Review 3
U14	Present Simple: Negatives	U14	Review 3	U14	Past: Be Verbs
U15	Present Simple: Questions	U15	Present Continuous: Positives	U15	Past: Regular Verbs
U16	Review 4	U16	Present Continuous: Negatives	U16	Past: Irregular Verbs
U17	Modal Verb: Can/Can't	U17	Present Continuous: Questions	U17	Past: Questions
U18	Modal Verb: Can Questions	U18	Review 4	U18	Review 4
U19	Review 5	U19	Modal Verb: Can / May	U19	Wh- Question: What, Who, Whose, Where, and When
U20	Wh- Question: What and Who	U20	Wh- Question: What, Who, and Whose	U20	Adjectives and Adverbs
U21	Prepositions of Place	U21	Prepositions of Time	U21	Comparatives
U22	Review 6	U22	Review 5	U22	Review 5

Background Music Copyright Details

- Waltz For A Child(왈츠 포 어 차일드), 김재영, 공유마당, CC BY
- Walking, 김현정, 공유마당, 자유이용
- (파트)part4-29 (리벨리 도 레 부아)Reveil dans les bois(숲속의 아침), 이철희, 공유마당, CC BY
- 아침(Morning), 계한용, 구재영, 공유마당, CC BY

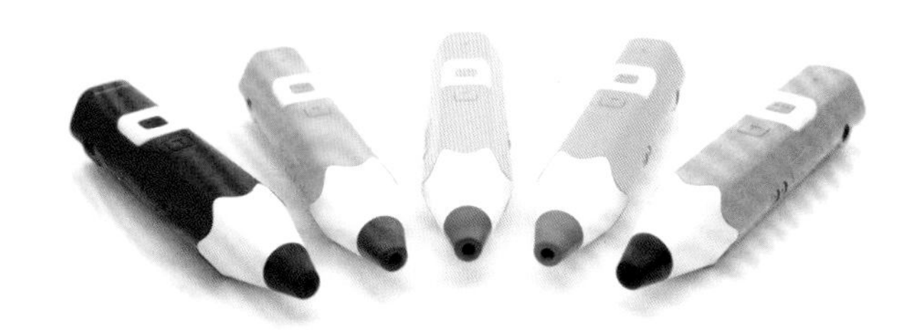

with 세이펜 SAYPEN TV

원어민 발음을 실시간 반복학습 — 단어 및 예문의 우리말 해석 듣기 — 혼자서도 쉽게 정답 확인 가능

세이펜 핀파일 다운로드 안내

STEP ① 세이펜과 컴퓨터를 USB 케이블로 연결하세요.

STEP ② 쎄듀북 홈페이지(www.cedubook.com)에 접속 후, 학습자료실 메뉴에서 학습할 교재를 찾아 이동합니다.

> 초등교재 ▶ ELT ▶ 학습교재 클릭 ▶ 세이펜 핀파일 자료 클릭
> ▶ 다운로드 (저장을 '다른 이름으로 저장'으로 변경하여 저장소를 USB로 변경) ▶ 완료

STEP ③ 음원 다운로드가 완료되면 세이펜과 컴퓨터의 USB 케이블을 분리하세요.

STEP ④ 세이펜을 분리하면 "시스템을 초기화 중입니다. 잠시만 기다려 주세요."라는 멘트가 나옵니다.

STEP ⑤ 멘트 종료 후 세이펜을 〈Oh! My Grammar〉 표지에 대보세요.
효과음이 나온 후 바로 학습을 시작할 수 있습니다.

참고사항

- 세이펜은 본 교재에 포함되어 있지 않습니다. 별도로 구매하여 이용할 수 있으며, 기존에 보유하신 세이펜이 있다면 핀파일만 다운로드해서 바로 이용하실 수 있습니다.
- 세이펜에서 제작된 모든 기종(기존에 보유하고 계신 기종도 호환 가능)으로 사용이 가능합니다.
- 모든 기종은 세이펜에서 권장하는 최신 펌웨어 업데이트를 진행해 주시기 바랍니다.
업데이트는 세이펜 홈페이지(www.saypen.com)에서 가능합니다.
- 핀파일은 쎄듀북 홈페이지(www.cedubook.com)와 세이펜 홈페이지(www.saypen.com)에서 모두 다운로드 가능합니다.
- 세이펜을 이용하지 않는 학습자는 쎄듀북 홈페이지 부가학습자료, 교재 내 QR코드 이미지 등을 활용하여 원어민 음성으로 학습하실 수 있습니다.
- 기타 문의사항은 www.cedubook.com / 02-3272-4766으로 연락 바랍니다.

세이펜과 함께 배우는 Oh! My Grammar

<Oh! My Grammar>는 Student Book에 세이펜이 적용되어 있습니다.
세이펜을 영어에 가져다 대기만 하면 원어민의 생생한 영어 발음과 억양을 듣고 영어 말하기 연습을 할 수 있습니다.
*****번역 기능** | 세이펜으로 책을 찍어서 원어민 음성을 들은 후, Ⓣ 버튼을 짧게 누르면 해석 음원을 들을 수 있습니다.

세이펜을 대면 유닛명을 들을 수 있습니다. Ⓣ 기능 지원

QR코드에 세이펜을 대면 해당 트랙의 MP3 파일이 재생됩니다.

세이펜을 대면 Christina 선생님의 우리말 문법 강의를 들을 수 있습니다.

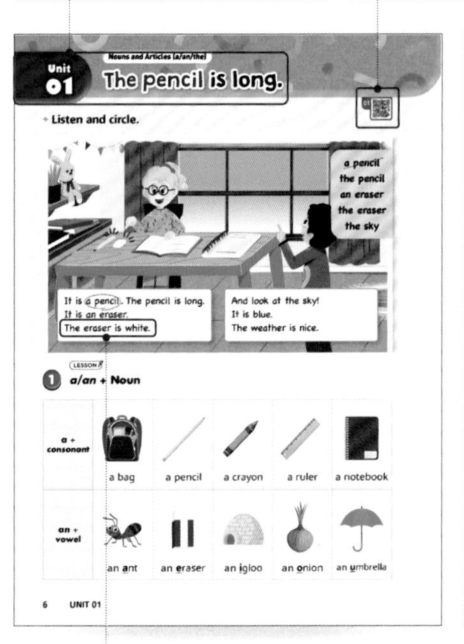

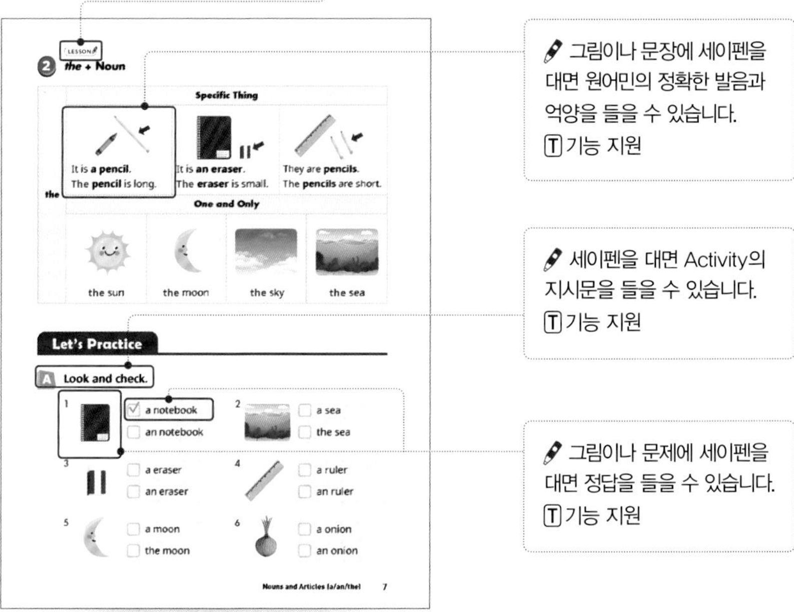

그림이나 문장에 세이펜을 대면 원어민의 정확한 발음과 억양을 들을 수 있습니다. Ⓣ 기능 지원

세이펜을 대면 Activity의 지시문을 들을 수 있습니다. Ⓣ 기능 지원

그림이나 문제에 세이펜을 대면 정답을 들을 수 있습니다. Ⓣ 기능 지원

문장에 세이펜을 대면 원어민의 정확한 발음과 억양을 들을 수 있습니다. Ⓣ 기능 지원

문제에 세이펜을 대면 정답이 포함된 문장을 들을 수 있습니다. Ⓣ 기능 지원

그림이나 문제에 세이펜을 대면 정답이 포함된 문장을 들을 수 있습니다. Ⓣ 기능 지원

세이펜을 대면 해당 영어 단어를 들을 수 있습니다. Ⓣ 기능 지원

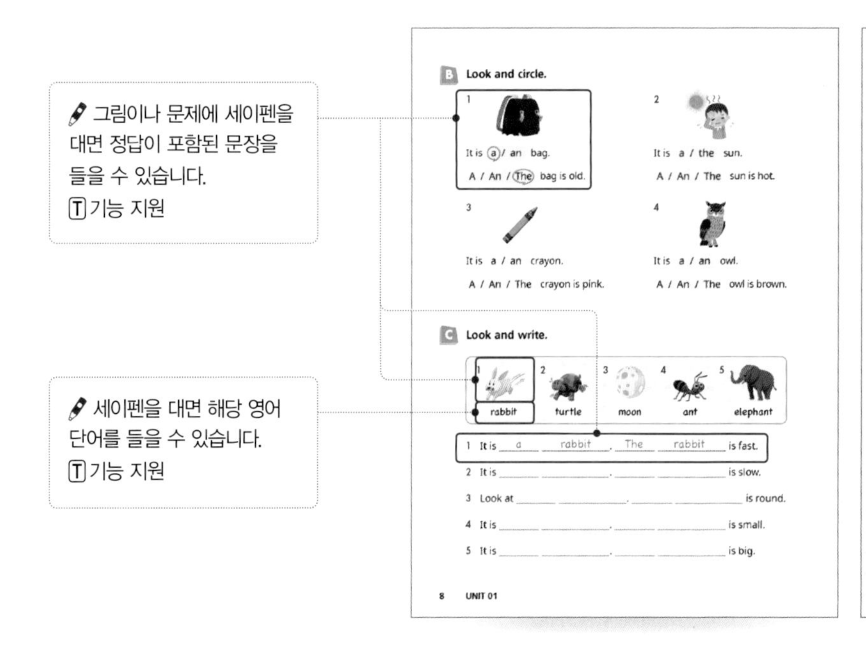

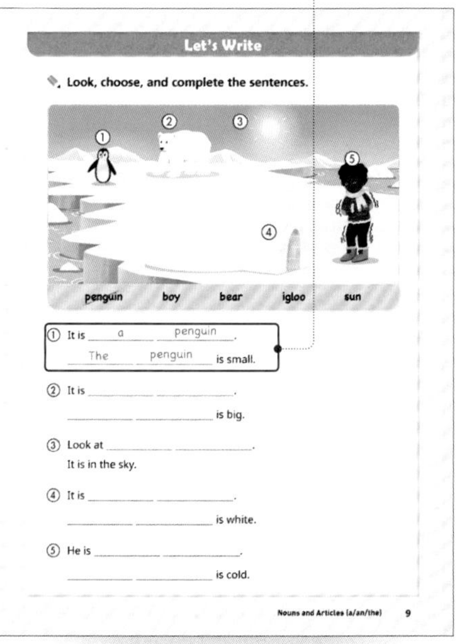

Oh! My Grammar 2

Workbook

CEDUBOOK

Oh! My Grammar 2

Workbook

CEDUBOOK

Contents

Nouns & Others

Be Verbs & More

Present Simple

Present Continuous

Modal Verbs & Others

Nouns and Articles (a/an/the)

Unit 01 The pencil is long.

Step 1 Write *a*, *an*, or *the*. Then, match.

1. It is ___a___ rabbit.
   ___The___ rabbit is fast.

2. It is ________ doll.
   ________ doll is pretty.

3. It is ________ apple.
   ________ apple is green.

4. Look at ________ moon.
   ________ moon is round.

Step 2 Look and write.

1. bag

   It is ___a___ ___bag___.
   ___The___ ___bag___ is old.

2. 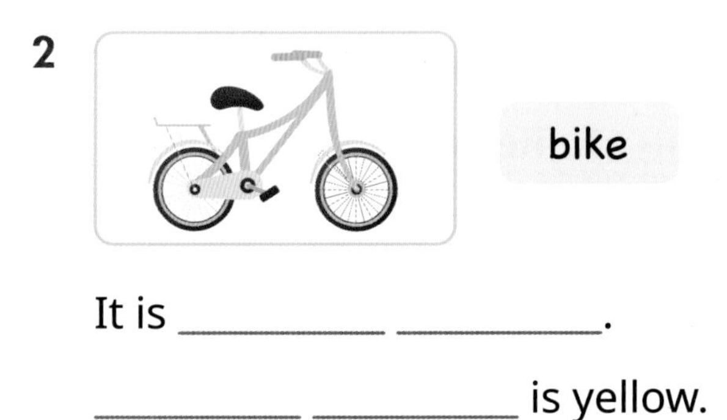

   bike

   It is ________ ________.
   ________ ________ is yellow.

3. 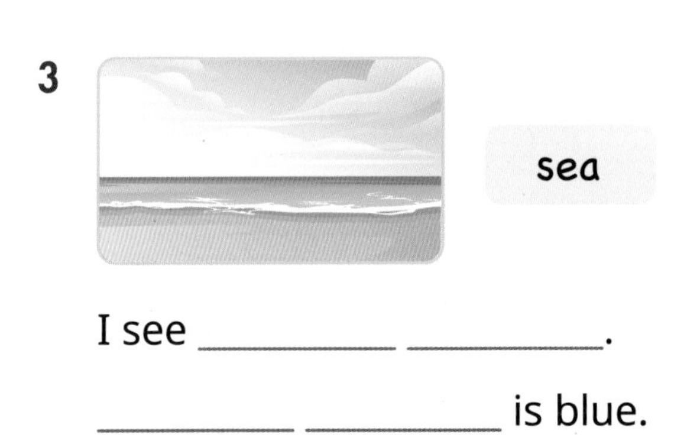

   sea

   I see ________ ________.
   ________ ________ is blue.

4. 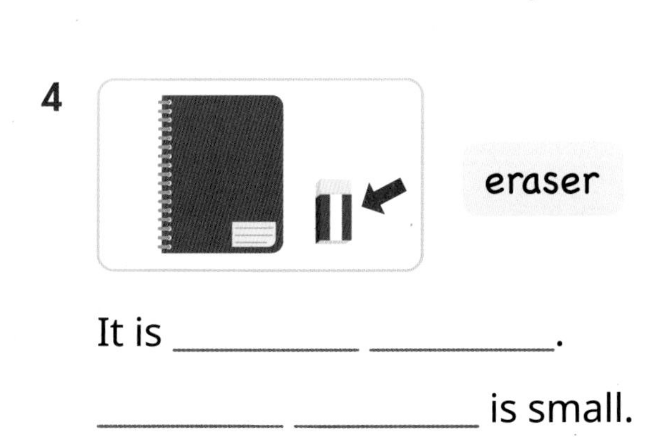

   eraser

   It is ________ ________.
   ________ ________ is small.

Step 3 Unscramble and write the sentences.

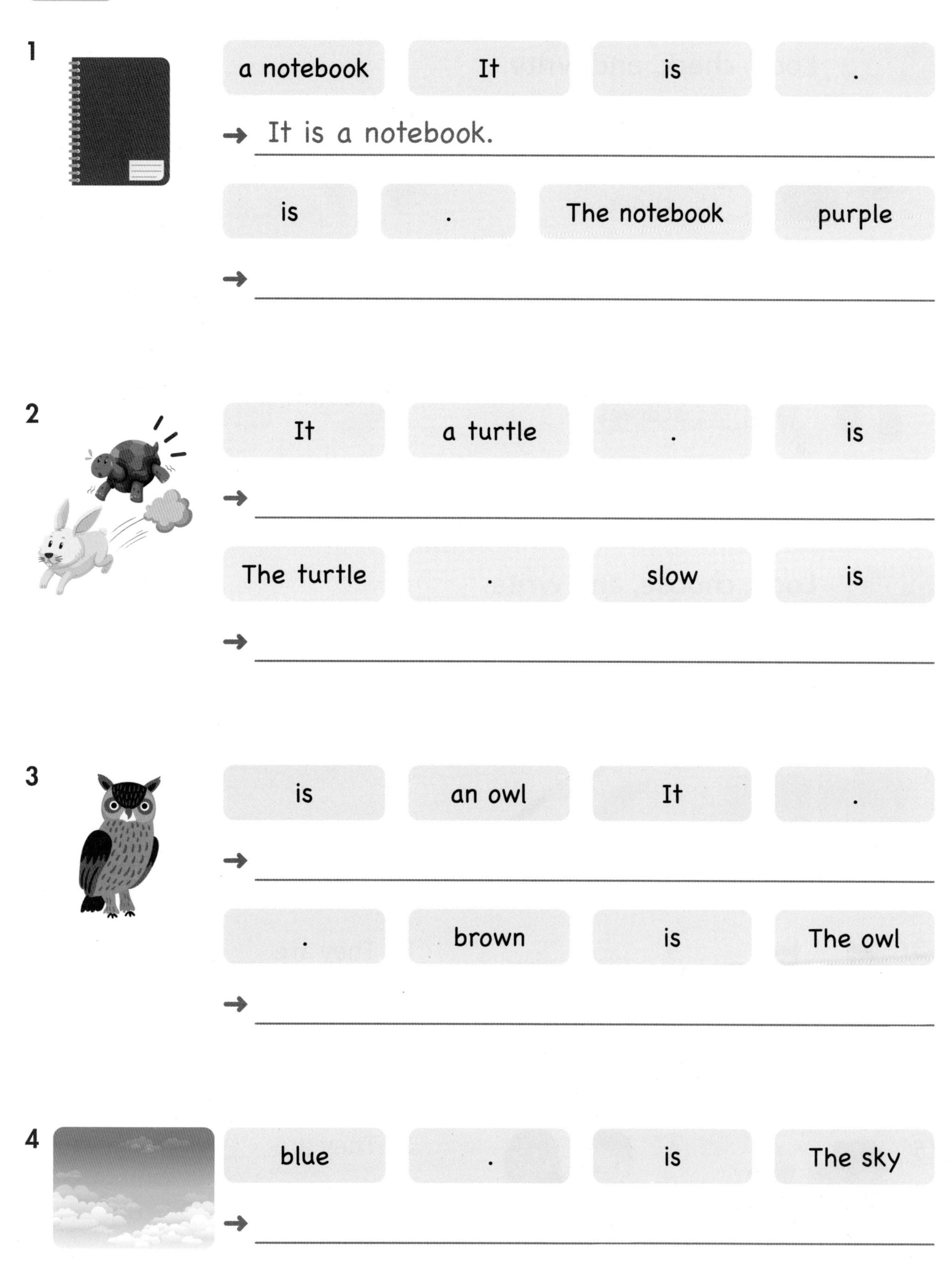

1

a notebook	It	is	.

→ It is a notebook.

is	.	The notebook	purple

→

2

It	a turtle	.	is

→

The turtle	.	slow	is

→

3

is	an owl	It	.

→

.	brown	is	The owl

→

4

blue	.	is	The sky

→

Plural Nouns

Unit 02 They are puppies.

Step 1 Look, check, and write.

1

- [x] cups
- [ ] cupes

They are cups.

2

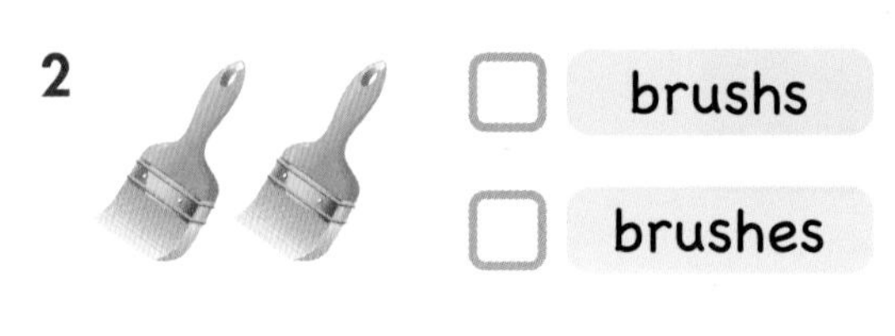

- [ ] brushs
- [ ] brushes

They are ________.

3

- [ ] scarfs
- [ ] scarves

They are ________.

4

- [ ] feet
- [ ] foots

They are ________.

Step 2 Look, choose, and write.

~~box~~	tree	baby	man	child	knife

① ② ③ ④ ⑤ ⑥

1 They are boxes.

2 They are ________.

3 They are ________.

4 They are ________.

5 They are ________.

6 They are ________.

Step 3 Look and rewrite in the plural forms.

1

It is a chicken.

→ They are chickens.

2

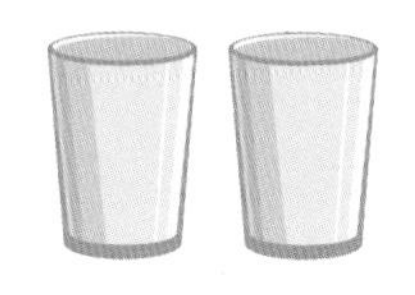

It is a glass.

→ ______________________

3

It is a mouse.

→ ______________________

4

It is a wolf.

→ ______________________

5

It is a puppy.

→ ______________________

6

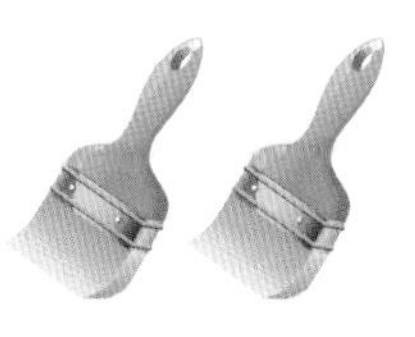

It is a brush.

→ ______________________

7

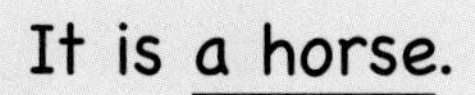

It is a horse.

→ ______________________

Unit 03 I want bread.

Step 1 Choose and write.

~~onion~~ bread egg banana water tea spoon sugar

Count Noun	Non-count Noun
onion	

Step 2 Choose and write with *a*, *an*, or *some*.

~~cookie~~ milk egg juice carrot peaches

1 I want a cookie.

2 He wants __________ __________.

3 She wants __________ __________.

4 He wants __________ __________.

5 I want __________ __________.

6 She wants __________ __________.

Step 3 **Look and circle. Then, write the sentences.**

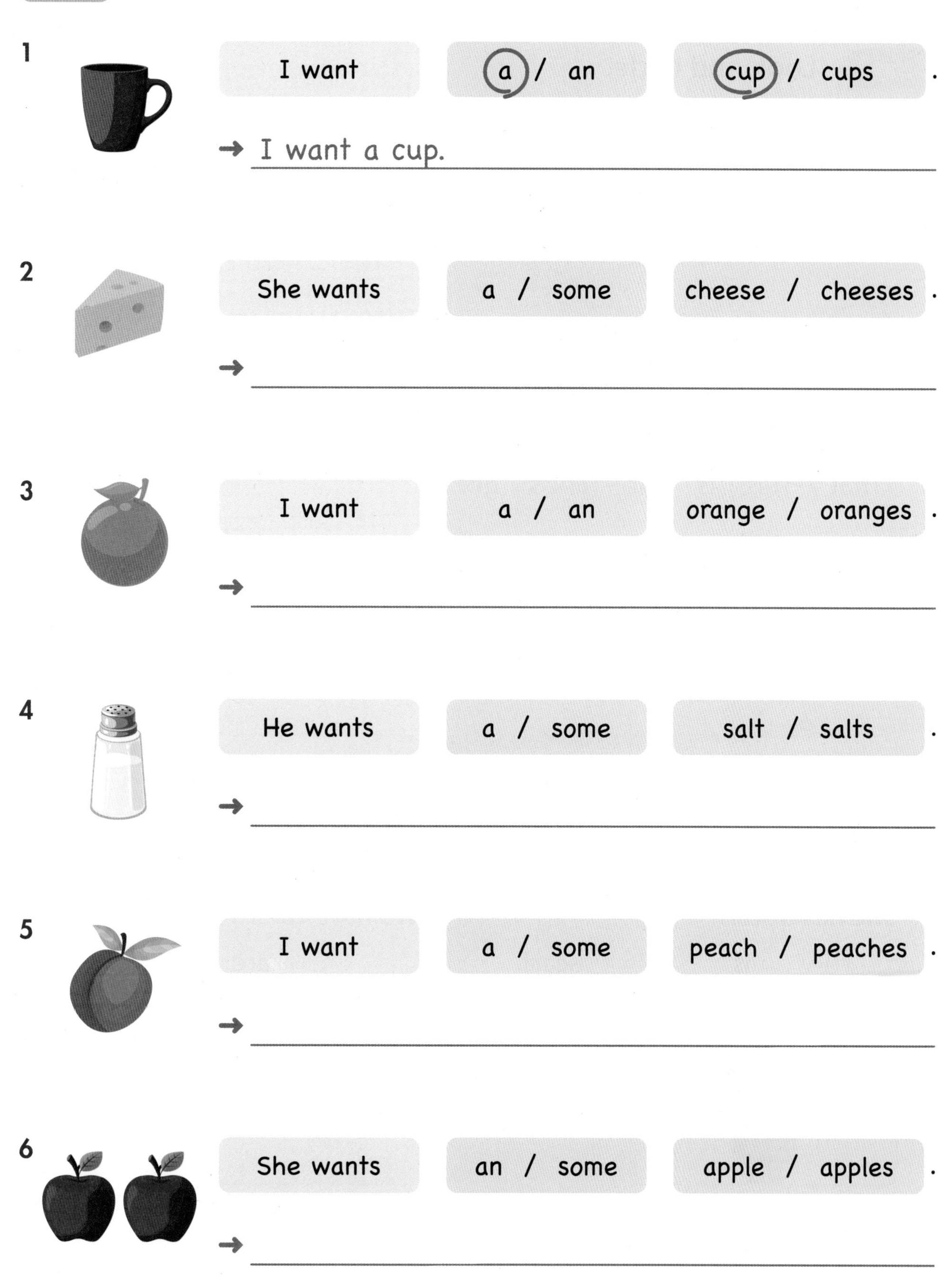

Demonstrative and Possessives

Unit 04 This is my watch.

Step 1 Look and circle.

①  ② 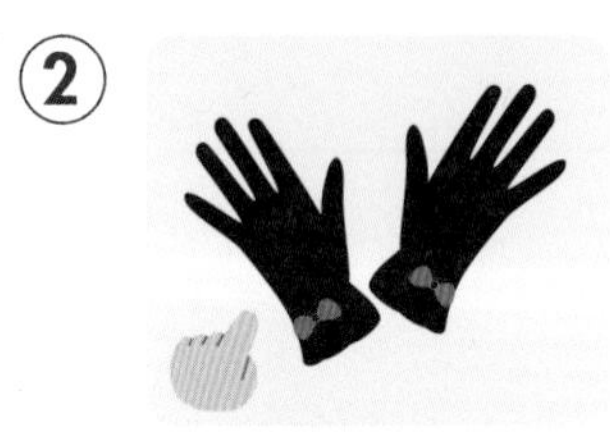 ③  ④ 

1 This / That is I / my house.

2 This / These are she / her gloves.

3 That / This is Eric / Eric's gift.

4 These / Those are they / their bikes.

Step 2 Look and write with *this, that, these,* or *those.*

1

Sue has a scarf.

That is Sue's scarf.

2

We have cars.

__________ are __________ cars.

3

He has gloves.

__________ are __________ gloves.

4

It has a fish.

__________ is __________ fish.

Step 3 Unscramble and write the sentences.

1

That	is	cat	.	my

→ That is my cat.

2

gifts	.	your	are	Those

→ ______________________

3

Kate's	are	.	boots	These

→ ______________________

4

That	school	our	is	.

→ ______________________

5

.	book	Mike's	is	This

→ ______________________

Unit 05 Review 1

✦ Unit 01-04 ✦

Step 1 Look, choose, and write.

a　　an　　the　　some

1 It is __a__ puppy.
__The__ puppy is small.

2 It is ______ sun.
______ sun is hot.

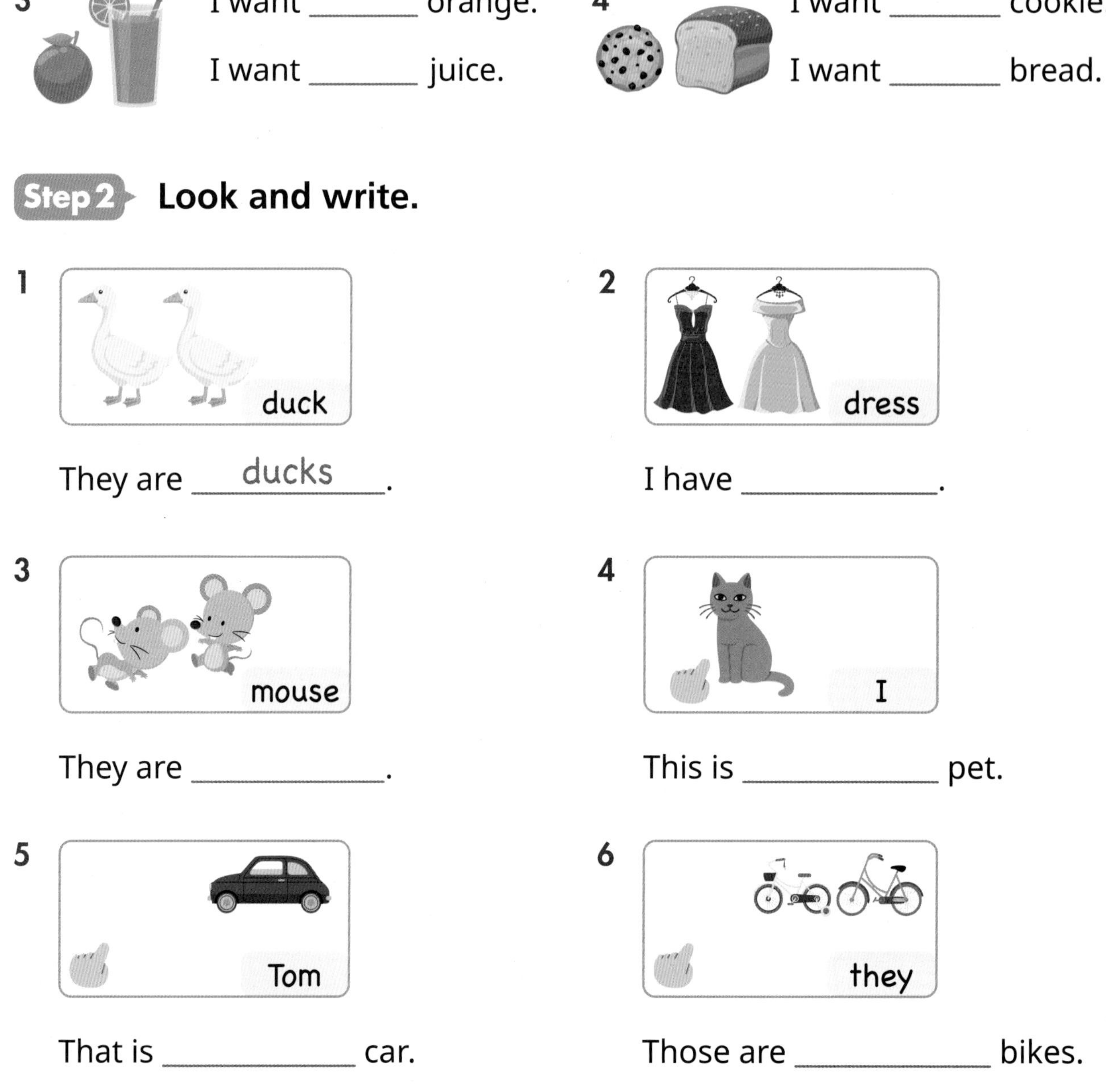

3 I want ______ orange.
I want ______ juice.

4 I want ______ cookie.
I want ______ bread.

Step 2 Look and write.

1 duck
They are __ducks__.

2 dress
I have ______.

3 mouse
They are ______.

4 I
This is ______ pet.

5 Tom
That is ______ car.

6 they
Those are ______ bikes.

Step 3 Unscramble and write the sentences.

1

a bear	It	is	.

→ It is a bear.

white	.	The bear	is

→ ____________________

2

.	a chicken	is	It

→ ____________________

They	wolves	are	.

→ ____________________

3

wants	She	.	an egg

→ ____________________

.	cheese	want	some	I

→ ____________________

4

.	hat	my	This	is

→ ____________________

These	her	are	.	boots

→ ____________________

Be Verb: Positives and Negatives

Unit 06 She is a singer.

Step 1 Look, circle, and write.

①  ②  ③  ④ 

1 Mason ___is___ a soccer player. He ___is not___ a baseball player.
am / (is) am not / (is not)

2 I ________ a bus driver. I ________ a pilot.
am / is am not / is not

3 Gina and I ________ singers. We ________ painters.
is / are isn't / aren't

4 It ________ a bike. It ________ a car.
is / are isn't / aren't

Step 2 Look and write.

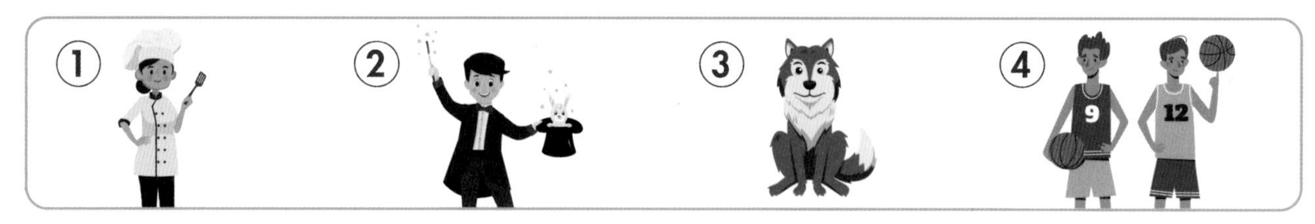

1 Nancy ___is___ a cook. She ___isn't___ a doctor.

2 You ________ a magician. You ________ an actor.

3 It ________ a wolf. It ________ a dog.

4 Tom and Eric ________ basketball players.

They ________ soccer players.

Step 3 Unscramble and write the sentences.

1

a vet	She	is	.

→ She is a vet.

.	isn't	She	a pianist

→

2

a television	It	.	is

→

.	not	a radio	is	It

→

3

We	.	are	scientists

→

doctors	We	not	.	are

→

4

.	are	frogs	They

→

They	iguanas	aren't	.

→

Be Verb: Questions

Unit 07 Is he tall?

Step 1 Read, write, and match.

1 ___Is___ Mark tall? — No, it isn't.

2 ________ you a firefighter? — Yes, he is.

3 ________ the turtle fast? — No, she isn't.

4 ________ the hamsters big? — Yes, I am.

5 ________ she old? — No, they aren't.

Step 2 Look and complete the dialogues.

1 ___Is___ Alice a magician? ___No___, ___she___ ___isn't___.

2 ________ you police officers? ________, ________ ________.

3 ________ the cat big? ________, ________ ________.

4 ________ they happy? ________, ________ ________.

Step 3 Unscramble and answer the questions.

1

Q Are you strong?

you / strong / Are / ?

A Yes, ___I___ ___am___.

2

Q ____________________

Is / fast / ? / the turtle

A No, ________ ________.

3

Q ____________________

? / young / Are / the children

A Yes, ________ ________.

4

Q ____________________

the girl / tall / Is / ?

A Yes, ________ ________.

5

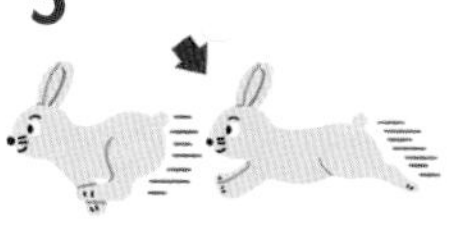

Q ____________________

Are / ? / slow / the rabbits

A No, ________ ________.

There + Be + Noun

Unit 08 There is a bench.

Step 1 Look and write *is* or *are*.

1 

There ___is___ a clock.

2 

There ______ flowers.

3 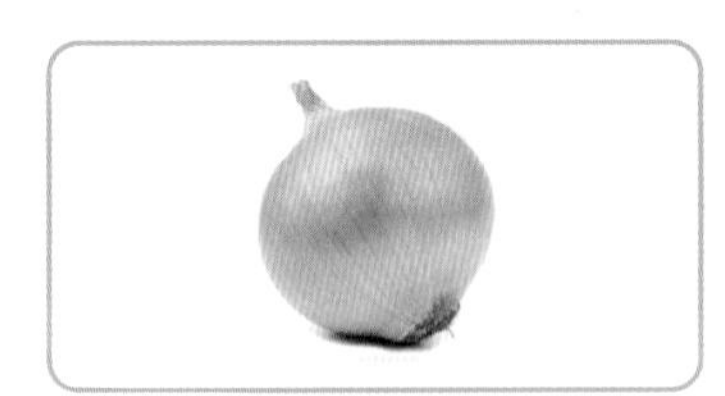

There ______ an onion.

4 

There ______ two carrots.

5 

There ______ four cows.

6 

There ______ a butterfly.

Step 2 Choose and write with *There is* or *There are*.

① ② 

③ 

④ 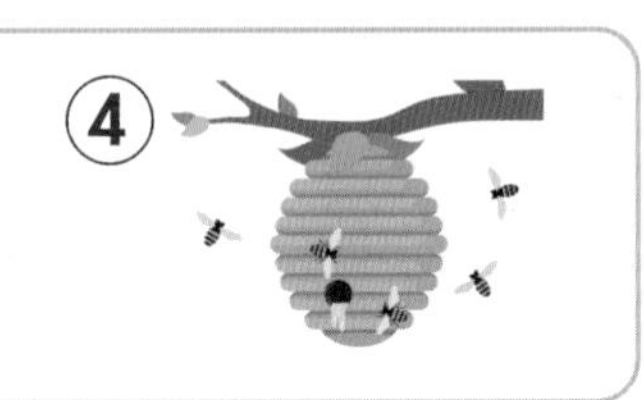

~~tables~~ bees lamp bird

1 ___There___ ___are___ two ___tables___.

2 ______ ______ a ______.

3 ______ ______ a ______.

4 ______ ______ five ______.

Step 3 **Look and circle. Then, write the sentences.**

1 There | (is) / are | (a sheep) / sheep .

→ There is a sheep.

2 There | is / are | a peach / peaches .

→ ______________________

3 There | is / are | a carrot / carrots .

→ ______________________

4 There | is / are | a mouse / mice .

→ ______________________

5 There | is / are | a bowl / bowls .

→ ______________________

6 There | is / are | an apple / apples .

→ ______________________

Adjectives

Unit 09 It is a new car.

Step 1 Look, circle, and write.

1

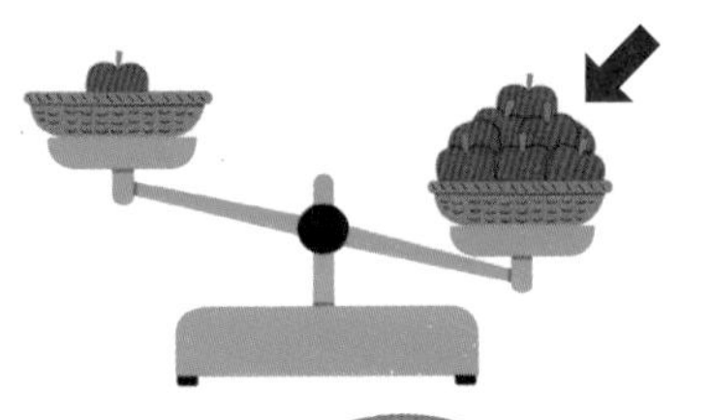

The basket is (heavy / light).

= It is a heavy basket.

2

The car is new / old.

= It is an ______ ______.

3

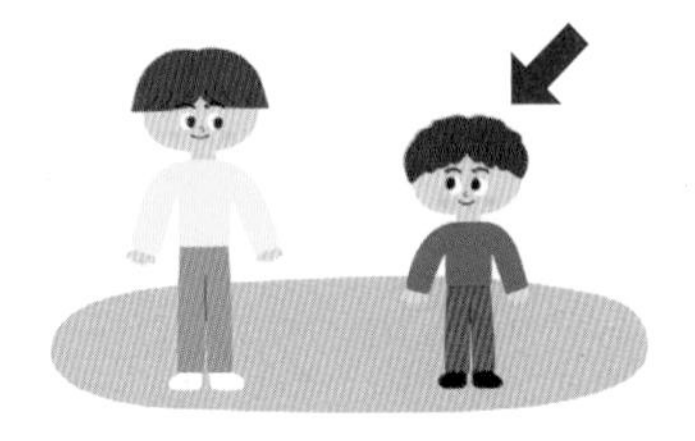

The boy is short / tall.

= He is a ______ ______.

4

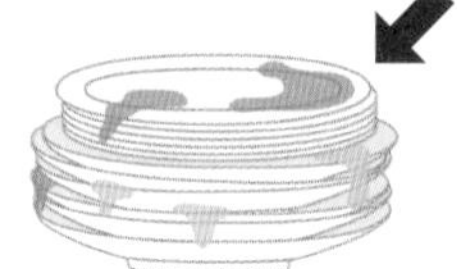

The dishes are clean / dirty.

= They are ______ ______.

Step 2 Change the sentences.

1 The apples are green. = They are green apples.

2 The river is long. = It is a ______ ______.

3 The shoes are new. = They are ______ ______.

4 He is a happy boy. = The boy ______ ______.

5 They are yellow leaves. = The leaves ______ ______.

6 The house is small. = It is a ______ ______.

Step 3 Unscramble and write the sentences.

1
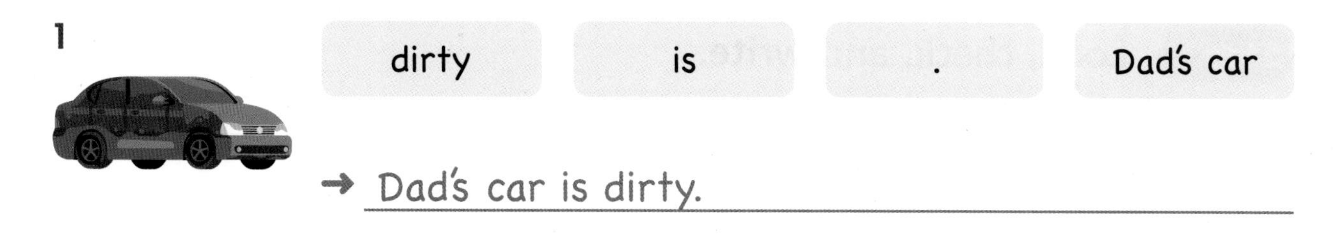

2
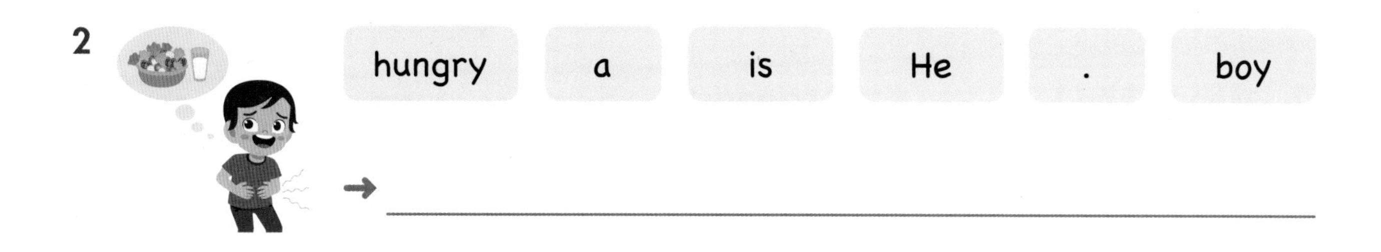

3

4
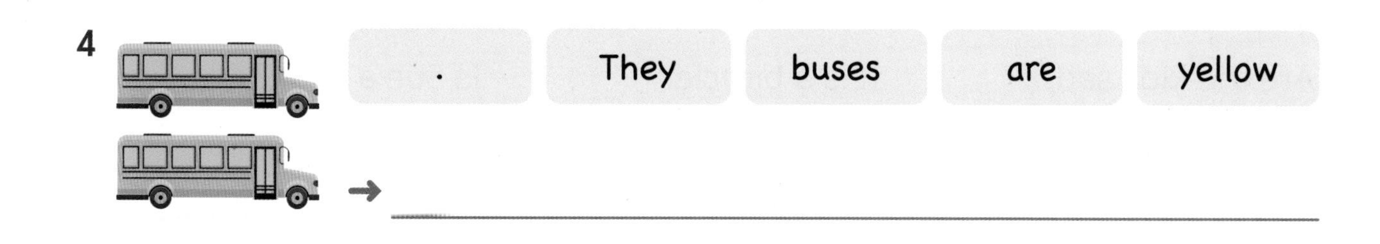

5
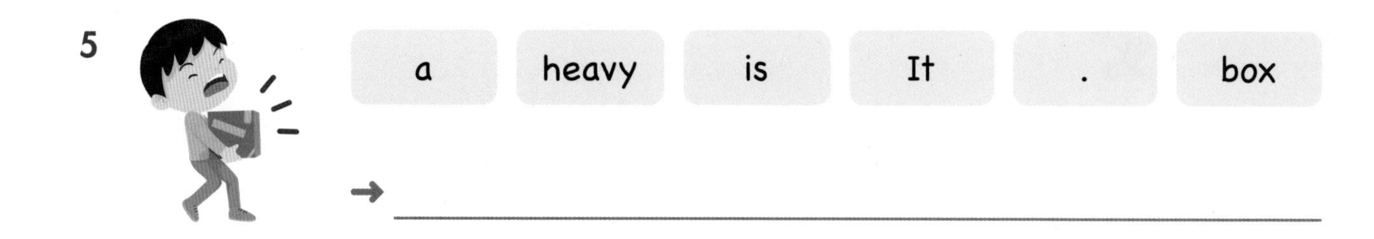

Unit 10 Review 2

✦ Unit 06-09 ✦

Step 1 Look, check, and write.

① 
② 
③ 
④ 

1 I ___am___ a police officer. ☑ am ☐ is

2 Megan and I __________ scientists. ☐ am ☐ are

3 There __________ a bench. ☐ is ☐ are

4 There __________ two peaches. ☐ is ☐ are

Step 2 Look and write.

1 

Are the kids sad?

No, ___they___ ___aren't___.

2 

It is a bicycle.

It __________ a car.

3 

Is Sue a cook?

Yes, __________ __________.

4 

The box isn't light.

It's a __________ box.

5 

The bus isn't blue.

It is __________.

6 

The dishes aren't clean.

They're __________ dishes.

Step 3 **Unscramble and write the sentences.**

1

She	.	is	my sister

→ She is my sister.

is	tall	.	My sister

→

2

.	is	a singer	He

→

He	.	isn't	a painter

→

3

.	a table	There	is

→

are	There	chairs	.

→

4

snakes	are	They	.

→

They	long	snakes	.	are

→

Unit 11 Tom has breakfast.

Step 1 Read, circle, and write.

1. do / (does) — He ___does___ his homework at 5:00.
2. study / studies — She ________ English every day.
3. have / has — The students ________ lunch at 12:30.
4. kiss / kisses — The dad ________ his baby.
5. drink / drinks — My mom ________ coffee every day.
6. wash / washes — They ________ the car on Sunday.

Step 2 Look and write.

1

go

Dad ___goes___ to work at 8:00.

We ___go___ to school at 9:00.

2

wash

Susan ________ her face.

They ________ the dishes.

3

sleep

The baby ________ at night.

The puppies ________ at night.

4

read

The man ________ a newspaper.

The children ________ books.

Step 3 Change the sentences.

1 I draw a picture every day.

→ He ___draws a picture___ every day.

2 Christina has dinner at 6:30.

→ We ______________________ at 6:30.

3 A bat flies in the sky.

→ Birds ______________________ in the sky.

4 Kate and Andy cook breakfast every day.

→ My mother ______________________ every day.

5 We watch television every day.

→ My dad ______________________ every day.

6 They teach English at school.

→ Mr. White ______________________ at school.

Present Simple: Negatives

Unit 12 They don't drink milk.

Step 1 Read and write *don't* or *doesn't*.

1 My brother ___doesn't___ brush his hair.

2 They ______________ fly the kites.

3 She ______________ eat meat.

4 Chris ______________ have a pet.

5 Brian and I ______________ like carrots.

Step 2 Look and write the correct forms of the verbs.

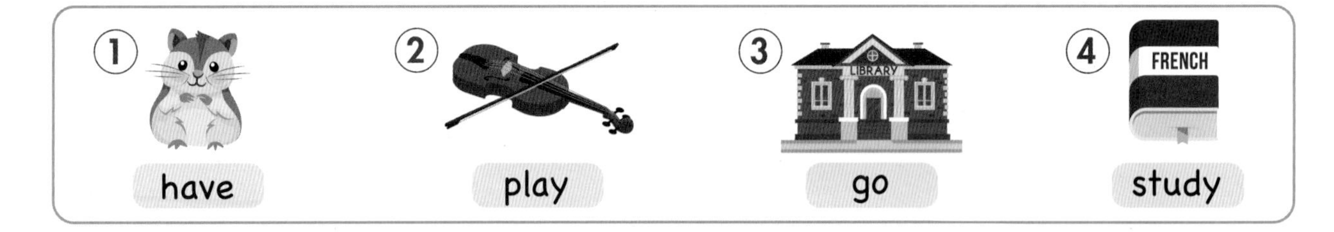

1 I ___have___ a hamster.

I ___don't___ ___have___ a cat.

2 Nick ______________ the violin.

He ______________ ______________ the piano.

3 My sister ______________ to the library.

She ______________ ______________ to the playground.

4 They ______________ French.

They ______________ ______________ English.

Step 3 Look, circle, and unscramble.

1

don't / doesn't	make	cookies	I	.

→ I don't make cookies.

2

don't / doesn't	Sean	math	study	.

→ ____________________

3

don't / doesn't	drink	The girl	milk	.

→ ____________________

4

don't / doesn't	salads	eat	They	.

→ ____________________

5

don't / doesn't	have	A bird	arms	.

→ ____________________

Present Simple: Questions

Unit 13 Does he play soccer?

Step 1 Look, write, and circle.

1 ___Do___ they dance? Yes, (they do) / they does .

2 ________ you play basketball? No, I don't / I doesn't .

3 ________ the bird sing? Yes, it do / it does .

4 ________ the girl watch TV? No, she don't / she doesn't .

Step 2 Look and complete the dialogues.

Every Day	ride a bike	cook dinner	take a shower	do the dishes
Ann	O	X	X	O
Sam	X	O	O	O

1 ___Does___ Ann ride a bike? ___Yes___, ___she___ ___does___.

2 ________ Ann cook dinner? ________, ________ ________.

3 ________ Sam take a shower? ________, ________ ________.

4 ________ Ann and Sam do the dishes? ________, ________ ________.

Step 3 Unscramble and write the questions.

1

Q Does he dance?

Does / dance / ? / he

A No, he doesn't.

2

Q ______________________________

a book / ? / you / read / Do

A No, I don't.

3

Q ______________________________

? / paint / Does / Amy / a picture

A Yes, she does.

4

Q ______________________________

Do / a school bus / ? / take / they

A Yes, they do.

5

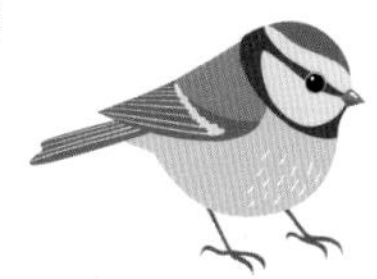

Q ______________________________

a bird / have / Does / wings / ?

A Yes, it does.

Unit 14 Review 3

✦ Unit 11-13 ✦

Step 1 Read, circle, and write.

1 (sleep) sleeps — The babies ___sleep___ on the bed.

2 teachs teaches — He ________ math at school.

3 don't doesn't — My mom ________ drink coffee.

4 don't doesn't — They ________ watch TV every day.

5 have has — Lucy ________ breakfast every day.

Step 2 Look and write.

Every Day	make dinner	do the dishes	exercise	study Chinese
I	O	X	X	X
Emily	X	O	O	O

1 I ___make___ dinner. Emily ___doesn't___ ___make___ dinner.

2 Emily ________ the dishes. I ________ ________ the dishes.

3 ________ you exercise? ________, ________ ________.

4 ________ Emily study Chinese? ________, ________ ________.

Step 3 Correct the mistakes and rewrite.

1

She wash her face every day.

→ She washes her face every day.

2

My brother don't play the guitar.

→ ______________________________

3

Snails don't has legs.

→ ______________________________

4

Do they goes to school every day?

→ ______________________________

5

The birds flies in the sky.

→ ______________________________

Present Continuous: Positives

Unit 15 The girl is dancing.

Step 1 Read, circle, and write.

1 I (am) / is cooking now. — cook

2 He am / is ______________ on the sofa now. — sit

3 They is / are ______________ letters now. — write

4 Kate is / are ______________ a picture now. — draw

5 My mother is / are ______________ the kitchen now. — clean

6 Megan and I am / are ______________ lunch now. — eat

Step 2 Look, choose, and write.

~~sing~~ read swim dance ride run

①

②

③

④

⑤

⑥

1 He is singing now.

2 I __________ ______________ a horse.

3 We __________ ______________ books.

4 The dog __________ ______________.

5 The girls __________ ______________.

6 They __________ ______________ now.

Step 3 Unscramble and write the sentences.

1

My father	.	cooking	is

→ My father is cooking.

2

is	The cat	sleeping	.

→ ______________________

3

They	.	on the bench	are	sitting

→ ______________________

4

riding	.	is	He	a bike

→ ______________________

5

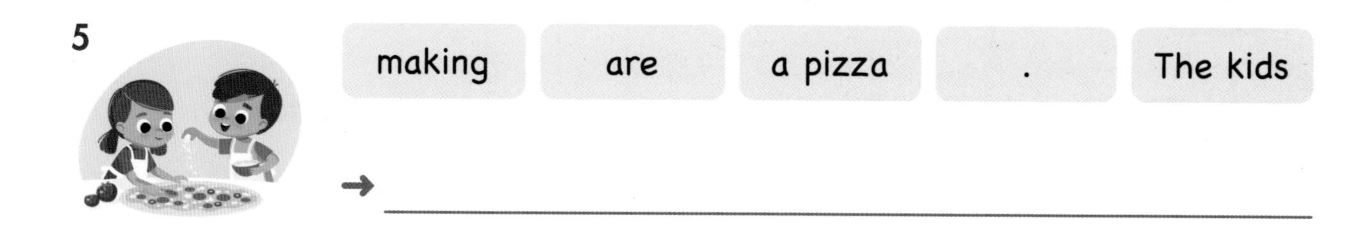

making	are	a pizza	.	The kids

→ ______________________

Present Continuous: Negatives

Unit 16 The woman isn't sitting.

Step 1 Look, circle, and write.

1 My brother (isn't) / aren't doing his homework now.

2 They isn't / aren't ______ now.

3 She isn't / aren't ______ a letter now.

4 The birds isn't / aren't ______ now.

Step 2 Look and write the correct forms of the verbs.

1
listen — The boy is listening to music.
read — He isn't reading a book.

2
sit — They ______ ______ on a bench.
stand — They ______ ______.

3
walk — We ______ ______ in the park.
run — We ______ ______.

4
sleep — The cat ______ ______ now.
play — It ______ ______ with a toy.

Step 3 Unscramble and write the sentences.

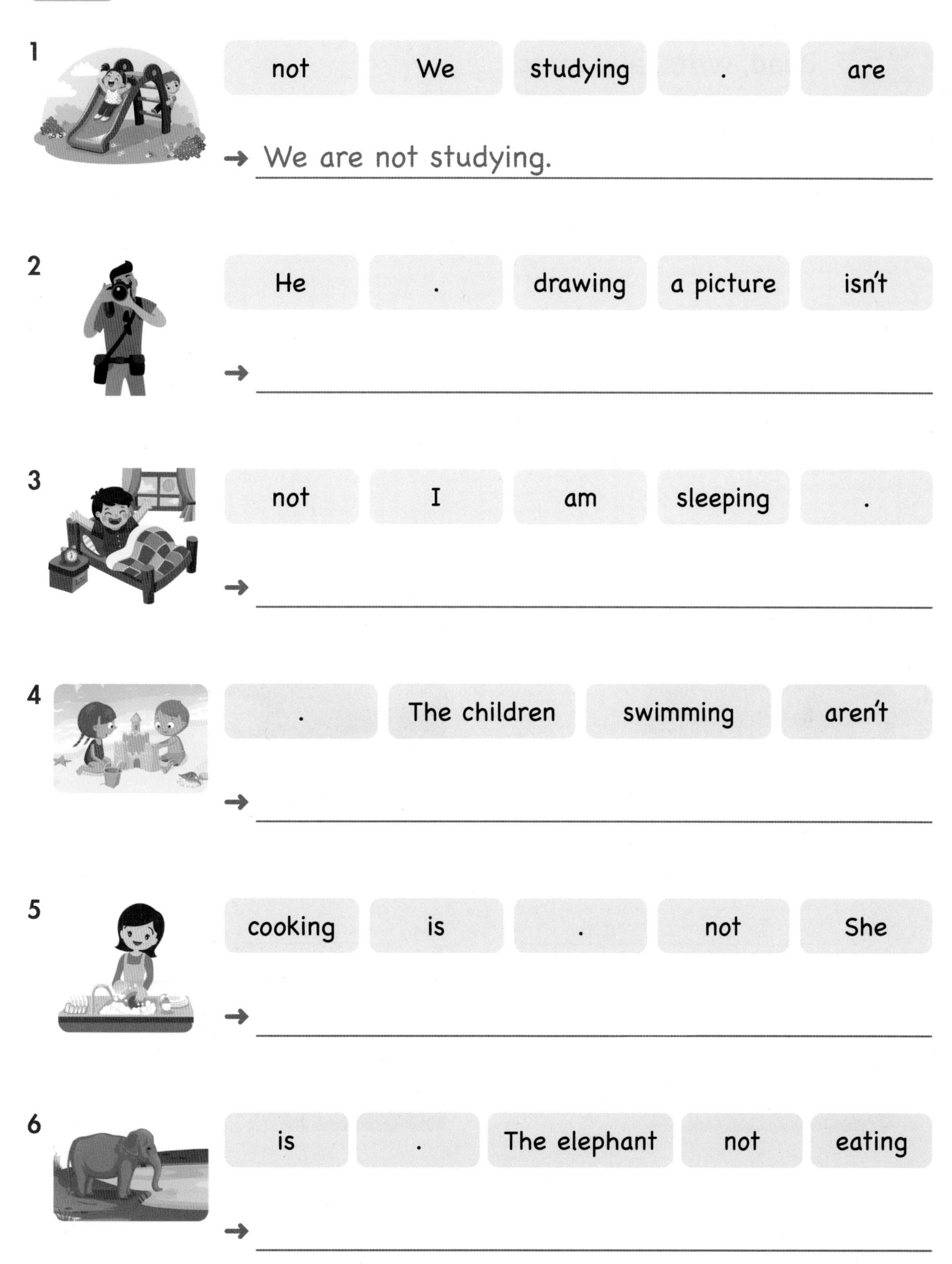

1 not / We / studying / . / are

→ We are not studying.

2 He / . / drawing / a picture / isn't

→ ______________________________

3 not / I / am / sleeping / .

→ ______________________________

4 . / The children / swimming / aren't

→ ______________________________

5 cooking / is / . / not / She

→ ______________________________

6 is / . / The elephant / not / eating

→ ______________________________

Present Continuous: Questions

Unit 17 Are you reading?

Step 1 Read, write, and match.

1 ___Is___ she riding a bike? — Yes, she is.

2 ________ you eating breakfast?

3 ________ the duck swimming?

4 ________ the kids laughing?

5 ________ he cutting the grass?

No, he isn't.

Yes, she is.

No, it isn't.

Yes, I am.

Yes, they are.

Step 2 Look and complete the dialogues.

1

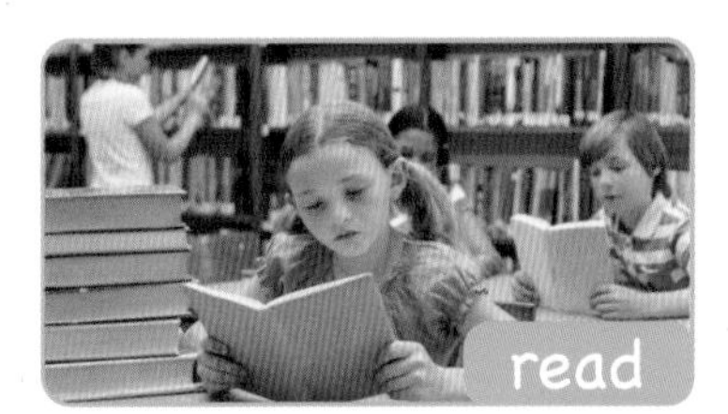

read

___Are___ you ___reading___?

Yes, ___I___ ___am___.

2

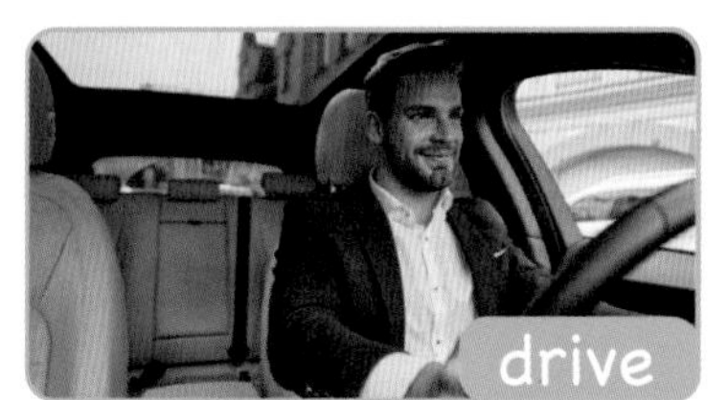

drive

________ Ted ________ a car?

Yes, ________ ________.

3

run

________ she ________?

No, ________ ________.

4

dance

________ they ________?

Yes, ________ ________.

Step 3 Unscramble and write the questions.

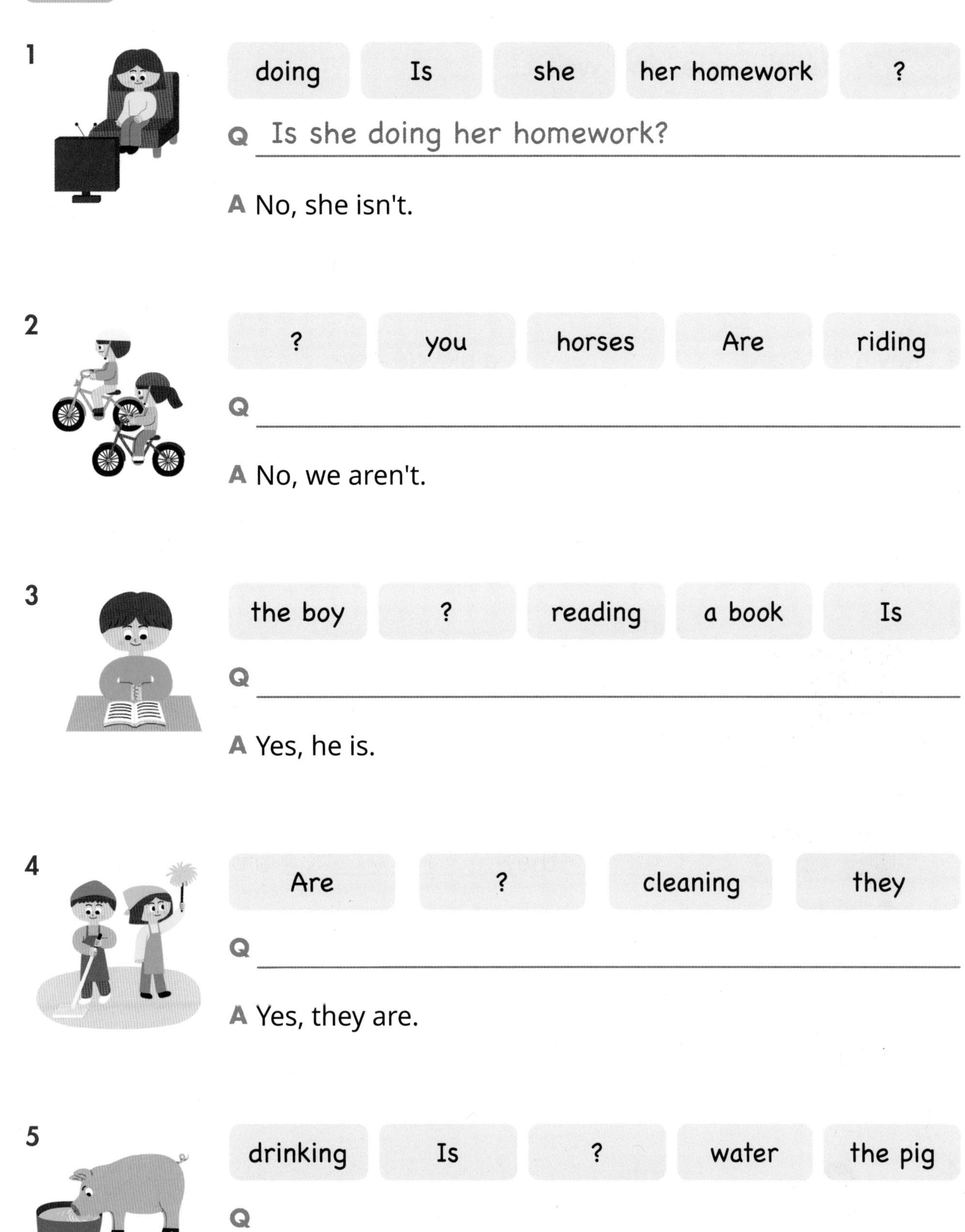

1

doing	Is	she	her homework	?

Q Is she doing her homework?

A No, she isn't.

2

?	you	horses	Are	riding

Q ______________________

A No, we aren't.

3

the boy	?	reading	a book	Is

Q ______________________

A Yes, he is.

4

Are	?	cleaning	they

Q ______________________

A Yes, they are.

5

drinking	Is	?	water	the pig

Q ______________________

A Yes, it is.

Unit 18 Review 4

✦ Unit 15-17 ✦

Step 1 Read, circle, and write.

1 They is / (are) ___playing___ soccer now. — play

2 Mary and I am / are __________ now. — swim

3 She isn't / aren't __________ to music now. — listen

4 Kevin is / are __________ a bicycle now. — ride

5 The cheetahs isn't / aren't __________ now. — run

Step 2 Look and complete the dialogues.

1

watch

___Is___ he ___watching___ a movie now?

No, ___he___ ___isn't___.

2

make

__________ they __________ a pizza now?

Yes, __________ __________.

3

drink

__________ the dog __________ water now?

Yes, __________ __________.

4

write

__________ you __________ in a diary now?

No, __________ __________.

Step 3 Unscramble and write the sentences.

1

washing	He	.	is	the dishes

→ He is washing the dishes.

2

the children	?	Are	dancing

→ ______________________________

3

sleeping	Is	the cat	?

→ ______________________________

4

are	on the bench	We	sitting	.

→ ______________________________

5

.	are	studying	not	They

→ ______________________________

6

isn't	.	Lina	a horse	riding

→ ______________________________

Unit 19 May I take a picture?

Step 1 **Look and write *can, can't,* or *may*.**

1 

Tina __can__ cook.

2

He ________ skate.

3 

You ________ use my phone.

4 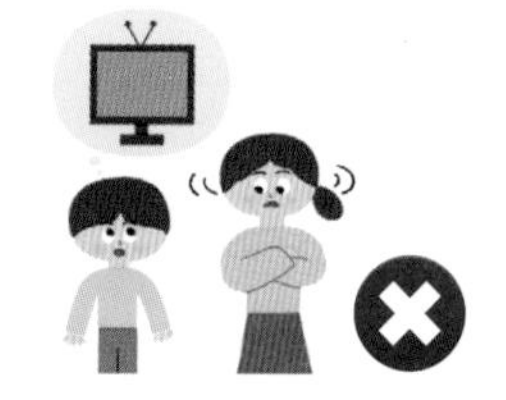

________ I watch TV?

No, you may not.

5 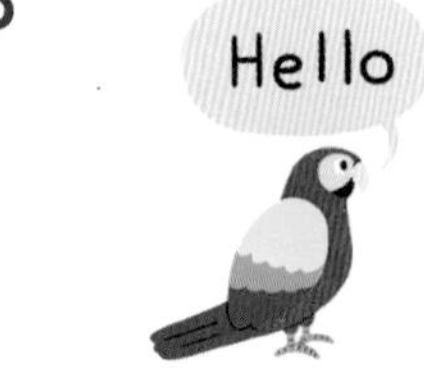

________ it talk?

Yes, it can.

6 

________ I have an apple?

Yes, you can.

Step 2 **Look and complete the dialogues.**

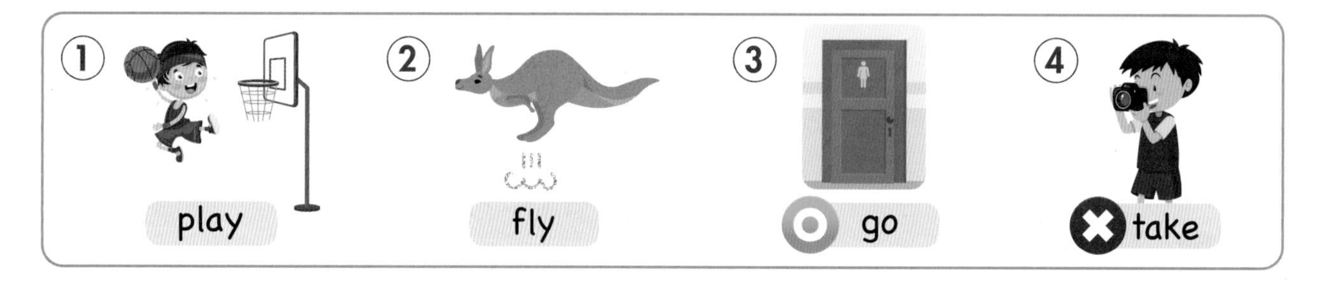

1 Can Sam __play__ basketball? __Yes__, he __can__.

2 Can a kangaroo ________? ________, it ________.

3 May I ________ to the bathroom? ________, you ________.

4 Can I ________ a picture? ________, you ________.

Step 3 Unscramble and write the sentences.

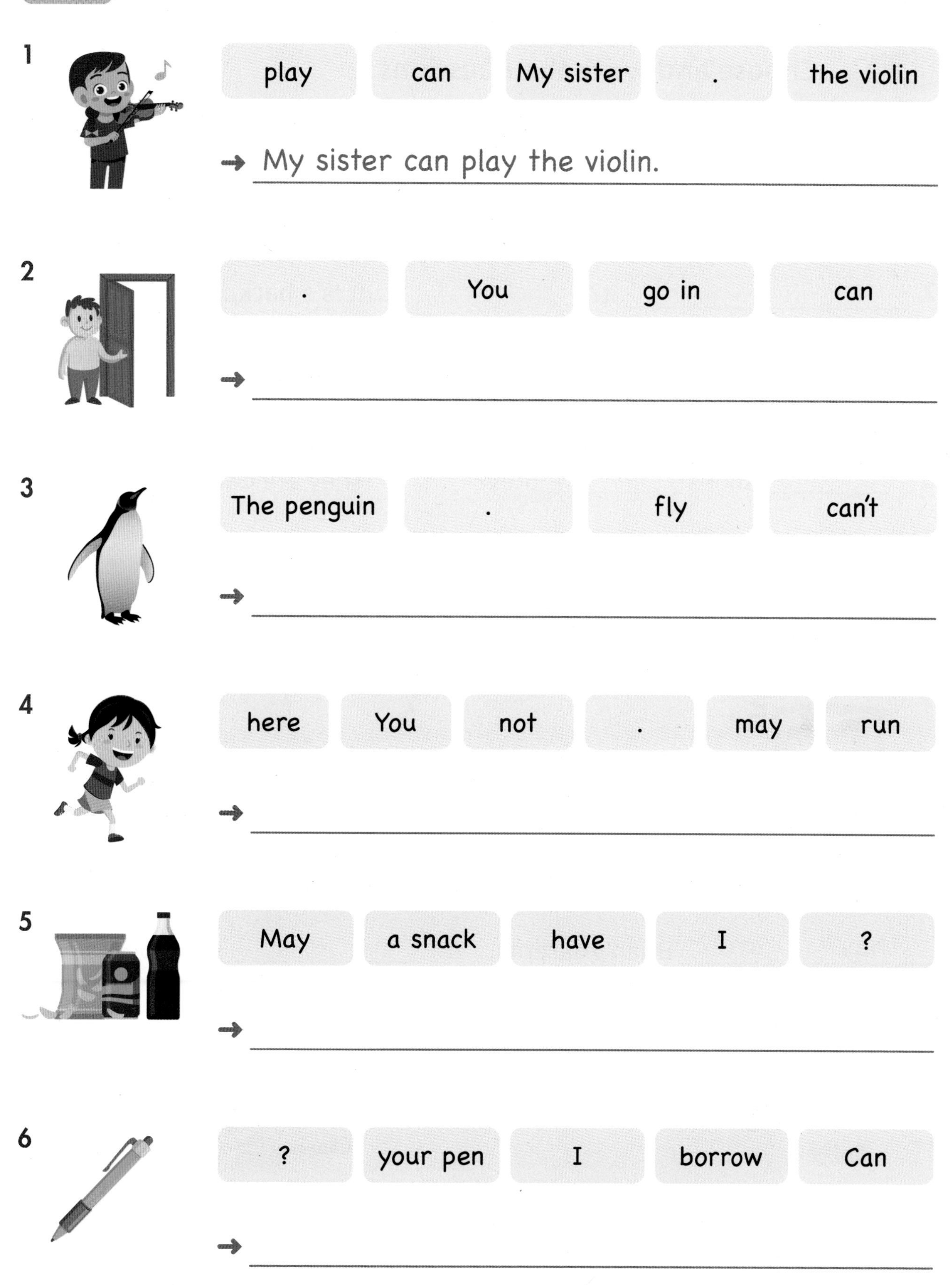

Unit 20 Whose jacket is it?

Step 1 Choose and write the questions.

who what whose

1 Who is she? She is May's sister.

2 ______ ______ it? It is a backpack.

3 ______ ______ you? We are Andy's classmates.

4 ______ ______ they? They are mittens.

5 ______ shoes ______ they? They are Carol's shoes.

6 ______ car ______ it? It is my dad's car.

Step 2 Look and complete the dialogues.

1

Who are they?

They are Brian's parents.

2

______ ______ they?

______ ______ boots.

3

______ ______ he?

______ ______ Sally's grandfather.

4

______ ______ ______ it?

______ ______ Clara's coat.

Step 3 Unscramble and write the answers.

1 

Q What are they?

they / What / are / ?

A They are jeans.

2 

Q ______________________

? / it / Whose / is / hat

A ________ ________ my grandfather's hat.

3 

Q ______________________

he / ? / Who / is

A ________ ________ Amy's brother.

4 

Q ______________________

are / glasses / they / Whose / ?

A ________ ________ Erin's glasses.

5 

Q ______________________

? / What / it / is

A ________ ________ a shirt.

Prepositions of Time

Unit 21 It is at 1 o'clock.

Step 1 **Read, match, and write.**

1 I have breakfast ___at___ 7:30. ·········· at

2 Halloween is ________ October.

3 Mom's birthday is ________ May 3rd.

4 Anne has art class ________ Tuesday.

5 I go to bed ________ 10 o'clock.

6 He goes to a soccer game ________ April.

at

on

in

Step 2 **This is Lucy's schedule. Look and write *at*, *on*, or *in*.**

1st week of September		
9/5 Thursday	9/6 Friday	9/7 Saturday
piano lesson 2:00 p.m.	go skating with friends 11:30 a.m.	Paul's birthday party 3:00 p.m.

1 Lucy has a piano lesson ___on___ Thursday.

The lesson starts ________ 2:00.

2 She goes skating ________ Friday.

She meets her friends ________ 11:30.

3 Paul's birthday is ________ September.

The party is ________ September 7th.

Step 3 Unscramble and write the sentences.

1

at	starts	7:30	.	The movie

→ The movie starts at 7:30.

2

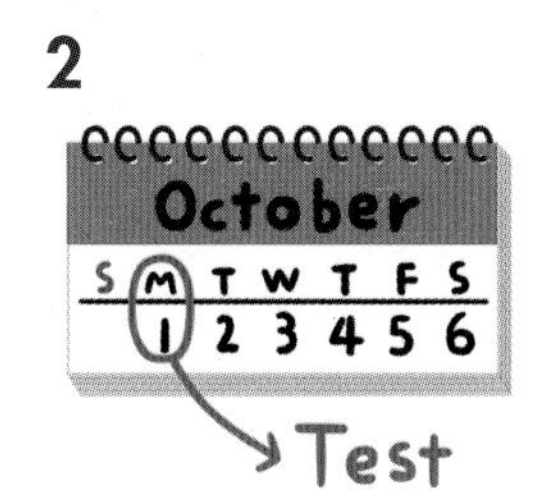

is	.	The test	Monday	on

→ ______________________________

3

in	is	.	Christmas	December

→ ______________________________

4

2 o'clock	at	is	The game	.

→ ______________________________

5

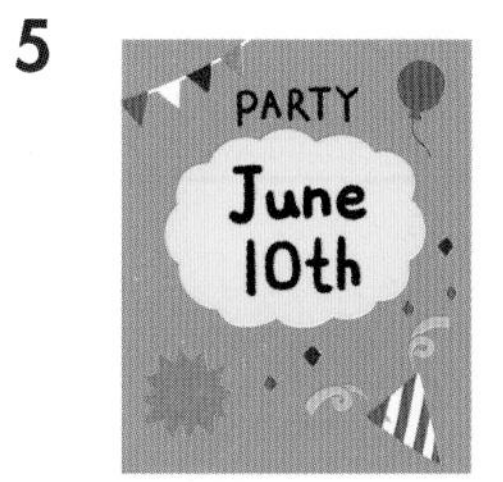

.	The party	June 10th	on	is

→ ______________________________

Unit 22

Review 5

+ Unit 19-21 +

Step 1 Read, choose, and write.

on	at	in		who	what	whose

1 When is the baseball game? It is ___on___ Friday.

2 ________ are they? They are mittens.

3 When is Grandma's birthday? It is ________ February.

4 When is the piano lesson? It is ________ 4:30.

5 ________ is she? She is my English teacher.

6 ________ notebooks are they? They are Mike's notebooks.

Step 2 Look and complete the dialogues.

① 

② 

③ 

④ 

1 ___Who___ ___are___ they? They are my parents.

2 Can Sam play basketball? Yes, ________ ________.

3 Can I take a picture in here? No, ________ ________.

4 ________ ________ ________ it? It is my uncle's car.

Step 3 Unscramble and write the sentences.

1 

Q Who are they?

are / Who / ? / they

A They are my brothers.

2 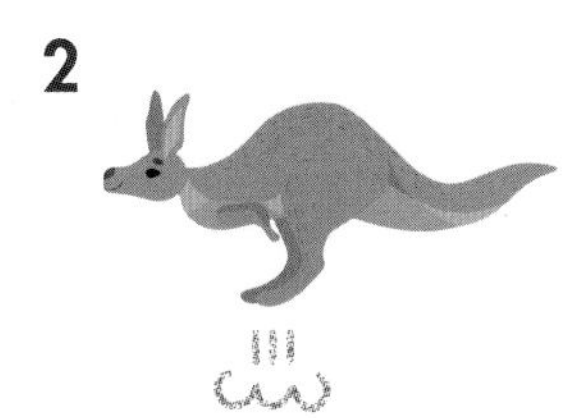

Q ______________________

jump / Can / a kangaroo / ? / high

A Yes, it can.

3 

Q ______________________

is / ? / Whose / it / hat

A It is my grandfather's hat.

4 

Q ______________________

? / have / May / I / a snack

A No, you may not.

5 

Q When is Christmas?

A ______________________

is / December 25th / . / It / on

Oh! My Grammar is a three-level grammar series designed for young students. *Oh! My Grammar* helps learners to easily understand basic grammar form, use, and meaning while also developing their writing skills. This series exposes students to natural English grammar so that they can learn how to use it in real-life situations. Learner-centered exercises enable students to use the grammar forms accurately and fluently. Interesting writing tasks and gradual sentence pattern practice boost students' confidence in their writing skills.

Oh! My Grammar Series

문제에 세이펜을 대면 정답이 포함된 문장을 들을 수 있습니다. Ⓣ기능 지원

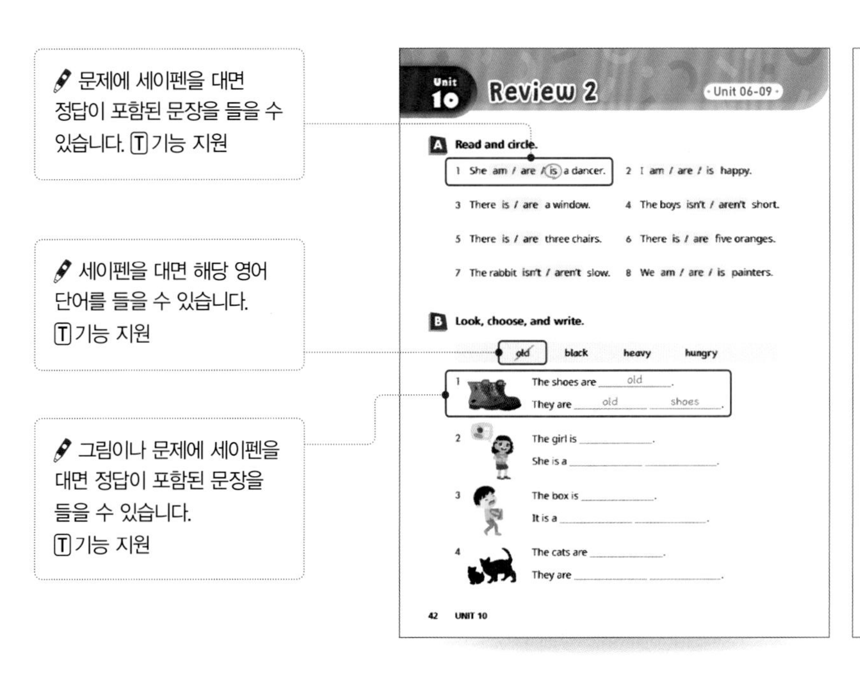

Unit 10 Review 2 · Unit 06-09 ·

A Read and circle.

1 She am / are / is a dancer.
2 I am / are / is happy.
3 There is / are a window.
4 The boys isn't / aren't short.
5 There is / are three chairs.
6 There is / are five oranges.
7 The rabbit isn't / aren't slow.
8 We am / are / is painters.

B Look, choose, and write.

old black heavy hungry

1 The shoes are old. They are old shoes.
2 The girl is ______. She is a ______ ______.
3 The box is ______. It is a ______ ______.
4 The cats are ______. They are ______ ______.

42 UNIT 10

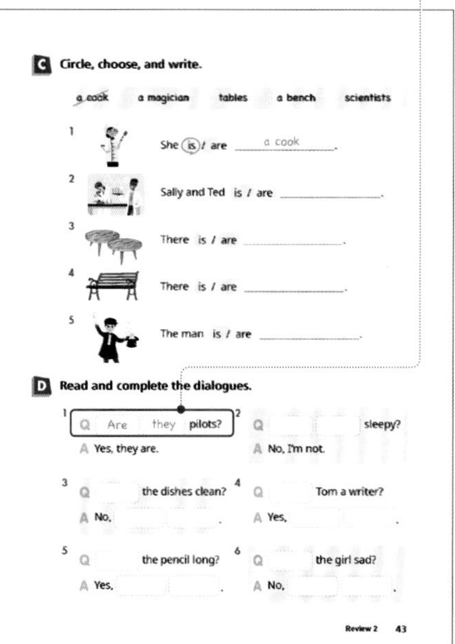

C Circle, choose, and write.

a cook a magician tables a bench scientists

1 She is / are a cook.
2 Sally and Ted is / are ______.
3 There is / are ______.
4 There is / are ______.
5 The man is / are ______.

D Read and complete the dialogues.

1 Q Are they pilots? A Yes, they are.
2 Q ______ sleepy? A No, I'm not.
3 Q ______ the dishes clean? A No, ______.
4 Q ______ Tom a writer? A Yes, ______.
5 Q ______ the pencil long? A Yes, ______.
6 Q ______ the girl sad? A No, ______.

Review 2 43

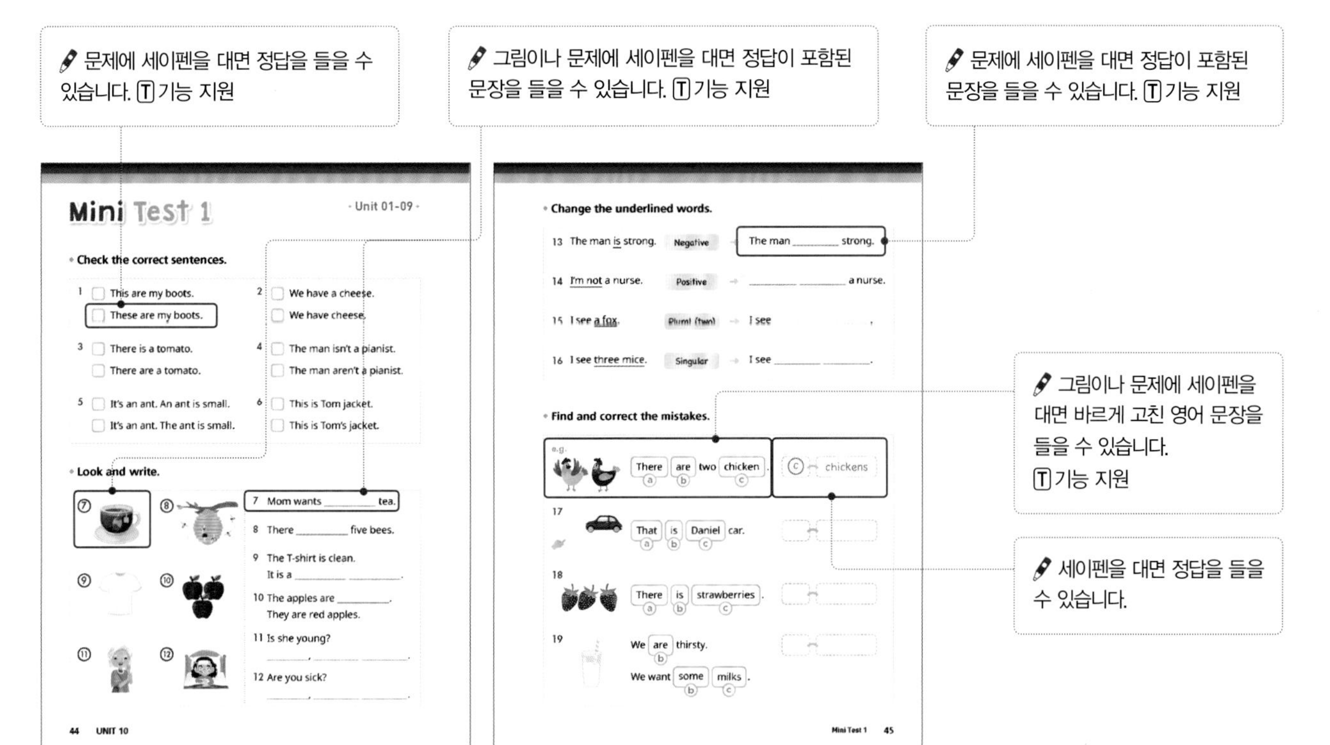

Mini Test 1 · Unit 01-09 ·

Check the correct sentences.

1 This are my boots. / These are my boots.
2 We have a cheese. / We have cheese.
3 There is a tomato. / There are a tomato.
4 The man isn't a pianist. / The man aren't a pianist.
5 It's an ant. An ant is small. / It's an ant. The ant is small.
6 This is Tom jacket. / This is Tom's jacket.

Look and write.

7 Mom wants ______ tea.
8 There ______ five bees.
9 The T-shirt is clean. It is a ______ ______.
10 The apples are ______. They are red apples.
11 Is she young? ______, ______ ______.
12 Are you sick? ______, ______ ______.

44 UNIT 10

Change the underlined words.

13 The man is strong. Negative → The man ______ strong.
14 I'm not a nurse. Positive → ______ ______ a nurse.
15 I see a fox. Plural (two) → I see ______ ______.
16 I see three mice. Singular → I see ______ ______.

Find and correct the mistakes.

e.g. There are two chicken. ⓒ → chickens
17 That is Daniel car.
18 There is strawberries.
19 We are thirsty. We want some milks.

Mini Test 1 45